A Love letter to the Mendonoma Coast

Sunrise Over the Coast

Craig Tooley

Mendonoma Sightings
Throughout the Year

by Jeanne A. Jackson
featuring the photographs of Craig Tooley

Mendonoma Sightings Throughout the Year

A month to month look at the fascinating world of Nature on the Mendocino/Sonoma Coast

Mendonoma Sightings Publishing
PO Box 1029
Gualala, CA 95445
(707)884-1760

ISBN: 978-0-615-95005-1

Cover photo: Craig Tooley
Cover design: Nanette Brichetto
Book design: Nanette Brichetto
Author photo: Craig Tooley
Photographer photo: Craig Tooley
Maps: Rixanne Wehren
Printing: Lorna Johnson Print

Printed in China

*To all who share their love
for the Mendonoma Coast
with me, this is for you.*

Table of Contents

Acknowledgments

I thank J. Steven McLaughlin, Editor and Publisher of the Independent Coast Observer, for giving me my start as a columnist, thus paving the way for this book. The support he and the entire staff of the ICO afford me is endlessly appreciated.

Many doors opened for me while this book was being created. For encouragement and advice I thank Rozann Grunig, Leslie Hoppe, Dan Wormhoudt, Lindsay Whiting, Linda Bostwick and Carolyn André.

For sharing their treasures of the sea - Abalone pearls - I thank Eric Anderson and Richard Lewis. Thanks to Mel Smith for getting up very early one morning so Craig Tooley could photograph his glass fishing floats.

Ron LeValley has the broadest nature knowledge of anyone I know. I was beyond fortunate to have him fact check this book. Along with fact checking, Ron allowed me to share several of his nature photographs. His generosity is amazing.

For editing and encouragement, Barry Richman, formerly of the McGraw Hill Book Company, was a godsend. He made the book better while our friendship deepened. I will be forever grateful. Breakfasts for life!

For those who shared their wildlife experiences, first in the ICO, and now here in this book, I feel blessed that you tell me your stories so I can spread the joy.

Many thanks to the accomplished photographers who allowed me to include their unique photos in this book. Their names can be found at the end of the book.

Craig Tooley's nature photographs bring you close to the splendor of the Coast. His eye for beauty is on full display here. It has been a joy collaborating with such a talented photographer.

To my husband Richard O. Jackson, who has been with me every step of the way, I give my thanks for his enthusiastic support of this book and for the love and life we share. We live in beauty together on the magnificent Mendonoma Coast. —Jeanne A. Jackson

I would like to thank Jeanne Jackson for asking me to collaborate with her on this book. Also, my soulmate, Rita, for her support and encouragement in my pursuit of photographic endeavors, and for sharing life and helping me find rapture in Nature, and viewing the world as extraordinary. —Craig Tooley

Spring

Perhaps you are here for a weekend, perhaps a lifetime. You can't help but make memories aplenty. From the surprise of the exquisite Calypso Orchids blooming in untouched forests to the miracle of the thousands of miles long migration of the Gray Whales, the Mendonoma Coast has it all.

Iridescent waves.

Craig Tooley

Mendonoma Sightings Throughout The Year

MARCH brings big storms but signs of spring are there for those who choose to see them. Rain and hail can be interspersed with dazzling sunshine, bringing the chance of rainbows. Rainbow days are one of the privileges we enjoy here on the Mendonoma Coast. Wild weather can also bring great surfing conditions.

Encounter with Big Waves and High Winds:

High surf caused by wind-driven storms and a high tide can make for a dramatic sighting.

"*Last Tuesday Jon and I were driving north on Highway 1, and just past Iversen Road we saw white things floating in the air that looked like clumps of really wet snowflakes. East Coast people know what that looks like. It was little bits of ocean foam that the wind was blowing up and onto the highway. Big waves and high winds joined together to inadvertently create a unique and smile-producing event. Lucky us to be passing by at the perfect time.*"

— Susan Sandoval, Gualala

Calm before the storm.   Jeanne Jackson

Sunset watching is a Coast tradition that crosses any boundaries that might divide us. With a storm on the way, the sky at sunset is magnificent.

When the storms abate, there can be fire in the sky – a meteor shower.

Spectacular Meteor:

Around 8 p.m. there was an impressive meteor that lasted an eternity – nearly five seconds. Mel Smith was at a friend's home on Fish Rock Road. He watched the meteor streak across the sky from the east.

It seemed to pass through Cassiopeia and then it broke into many pieces that glowed with white to reddish tones. As he watched, the light of the meteor fragments disappeared to the west, as if chasing the earlier sunset.

A Gray Whale, *Eschrichtius robustus*, submerges.   Craig Tooley

Wildlife Encounter with Gray Whales:

March is the perfect time to watch for Gray Whales on the Mendonoma Coast. The mothers with their calves are headed north and are very close in. Look for spouts, a big spout followed by a small one. It will warm your heart.

Later in the month there will be a different migration. Beautiful yachts will be seen sailing north, weather permitting. They are headed for Puget Sound in Washington, where they will be positioned for summer cruising.

" *Gregg Warner, my son Kiljan Cochran, and I were sitting enjoying a few relaxing moments after a day's work. We were looking out just west of the house and saw a family of Gray Whales breaching, blowing and playing together. The ocean was so windy, but the sun shining on the Whales was truly magnificent. It was one of those moments that made us so thankful to be alive!* " — Katy Warner, Gualala

Northern Flicker, *Colaptes auratus*, prefers
to find its favorite food, ants, on the ground.

Craig Tooley

Nesting birds are already building nests in cavities in snags – dead trees – in March. Unless they are a danger to your home, consider leaving these dead trees, as they are havens for many birds. They might also be used as seed trees by Woodpeckers or for drumming with their beaks to attract a mate. Some believe Woodpecker drums echoing off a tree are the heartbeat of the Earth Mother.

Northern Flickers are large Woodpeckers that inhabit the Coast year round. They are often found feeding on the ground, as they eat ants and beetles.

Fun Fact: Flickers are special birds to Native peoples. They particularly value them because these birds drum so well. If you have ever heard a Flicker using its beak to drum on a snag in the forest, you will understand. Native peoples believe that observing Flickers can teach you about communicating, music and joy.

Another Fun Fact: Flickers only use their nest hole once. Many other species of birds, Western Screech Owls in particular, and even some small mammals, will use old Flicker holes for their nests.

Young male Western Bluebird, *Sialia mexicana*.

Craig Tooley

Western Bluebirds begin "house hunting" in March, inspecting suitable birdhouses and tree cavities.

Wildlife Encounter with Western Bluebirds:

" *My wife, Gretel, and I discovered a pair of Western Bluebirds checking out two of our nesting boxes. First the male was leading his female partner to the boxes. She then flew into both boxes to inspect them. It is always the female Bluebird who decides and makes the final choice which box to use for the next generation of their young.* " — Siegfried Matull, The Sea Ranch

Black Trumpets, *Craterellus cornucopioides*, are easily overlooked on the forest floor.

Craig Tooley

Mushroom foragers continue to find Hedgehogs and Black Trumpets in March.

Fun Fact: Black Trumpets, which are also called Horn of Plenty, are hard to spot as they look like black holes in the ground. They are delicious in scalloped potato dishes.

Redwood Violets begin their long season of bloom in March. They are found along paths in the forest.

Redwood Violet, *Viola sempervirens*, kissed by raindrops.

Craig Tooley

Fun Fact: This wildflower is also called Evergreen Violet because the leaves are with us year round. But the flower has a very long life, blooming all spring and through the summer. It's our longest blooming wildflower.

Calypso Orchids are often spotted this month. These tiny, exquisite orchids cannot be easily transplanted as they are dependent on certain soil fungi, so please leave them be. You might discover some at Kruse Rhododendron State Reserve, on Kruse Ranch Road.

Fun Fact: Calypso Orchids can be difficult to spot as they are quite small. Look first for the slender, long leaf that is tapered at the end, growing on the forest duff.

Calypso Orchids, *Calypso bulbosa*.   Craig Tooley

Other wildflowers to look for this month are Milkmaids, Redwood Sorrel, California Poppies, and Hound's-tongue. Horsetails begin poking through the forest floor, in or near a stream. And nearby you might find lovely Western Trilliums.

Western Trilliums, *Trillium ovatum*.   Craig Tooley

Fun Fact: The blossoms are white when first up. As they age the flowers turn pink and finally purple. Never pick these wildflowers as they will take years to recover from the resulting lack of nutrients.

The big, beautiful leaves of the Fringed Corn Lily appear in March. This unique wildflower is endemic to the Sonoma and Mendocino Coasts. The flowers won't appear until summer when these leaves will be drying up. These plants grow near water.

Leaves of the Fringed Corn Lily, *Veratrum fimbriatum,*
a rare plant found only in Sonoma and Mendocino counties.

Craig Tooley

Brandt's Cormorant, *Phalacrocorax penicillatus*, in breeding plumage.

Craig Tooley

Pelagic Cormorants, seabirds, are returning to the offshore rocks and bluffs to begin their breeding season, as are Brandt's Cormorants. The male Brandt's Cormorant breeding plumage is beautiful to behold with his turquoise-blue throat patch.

A great place to see them is Gualala Point Island, which is visible from the bluffs on the south end of Gualala Point Regional Park. You can also traverse The Sea Ranch public access bluff trail from there to get an up close and personal look at this important offshore rookery.

Wildlife Encounter with Cormorants Flock Feeding:

" *I have been observing Cormorants in tight formation floating on the ocean, flock feeding. When I first observed this activity I thought I was looking at floating seaweed until it disappeared before my eyes and then reappeared a few seconds later. I ran to get my binoculars and found the 'seaweed' was a flock of Cormorants. I watched them again all dive in unison and reappear together.*" —Della Zita, Point Arena

A local bird expert, Richard Kuehn, explains this phenomenon.

" *It's very common behavior though it seems to increase this time of year as the Cormorants pair off and begin displaying. Many seabirds hunt cooperatively, even herding the schools of fish into a circle of their comrades. It is most amazing to observe. The American White Pelicans are very good at it too. Nature at its best!*"

Fun Fact: Brandt's Cormorants breed in colonies on offshore rocks. There is an established breeding colony on Gualala Point Island.

In March Ospreys begin to arrive, as they nest on the Coast.
Their piercing, beautiful calls signal the arrival of spring.

Osprey, *Pandion haliaetus*, and the moon.   Craig Tooley

Violet-green Swallow, *Tachycineta thalassina*, looking for a mate.   Craig Tooley

California Gulls leave the Coast in March to begin their spring migration to the plains of Montana and Southern Canada.

Violet-green Swallows – splashes of color flitting through the air – begin arriving. They will look for a dead tree for their nest or perhaps you will be lucky enough to attract them to that special birdhouse made just for them.

Wildlife Encounter with Violet-green Swallows:

" *On March 16 a group of Violet-green Swallows showed off their colors while flying over Del Mar Pool on The Sea Ranch just in time for St. Patrick's Day. They were chirping away almost as if to say, 'We're B-A-C-K...!'* "

— Barbara Gomes, The Sea Ranch

Lambs continue to be born in the flock that
works on keeping the grasses down at The Sea Ranch.
This young one has a very easy-going mother.

Lamb, *Ovis aries*, with its mother.   Craig Tooley

Jeanne's Wildlife Encounter with Butterflies:

March is when the California Tortoiseshell Butterflies normally pass through this area on their long migration northward.

" *They started arriving in the afternoon. Rick and I stepped out to take an afternoon walk and we were amazed to be surrounded by Tortoiseshell Butterflies. It was if a door had opened and they spilled out by the hundreds.*

" *We walked slower than usual because there were so many of them in the air. It felt as if we had entered a magical realm. We saw them feeding on the blossoms of our Manzanita, Ceanothus and English Laurel.* "

California Tortoiseshell Butterflies, *Nymphalis californica*.

Craig Tooley

Fun Fact: The California Tortoiseshell Butterfly in the middle has its wings closed, resembling a leaf, which is a defensive mechanism so it can hide in plain sight from its predators.

16

Male Anna's Hummingbirds keep working on their mating dance. The male will perch at the top of a tree, and then fly up, up, up. He then swoops down at high speed, pulling up at the last second to hover in front of his lady love. He makes a chirping sound, which comes from his tail feathers. Love is in the air!

Male Anna's Hummingbird, *Calypte anna*.   Craig Tooley

Fun Fact: Anna's Hummingbirds weigh about as much as a nickel. They are year round residents of the Mendonoma Coast. Native peoples hold this tiny bird in high esteem. One of their legends tells of Hummingbirds poking holes in the night sky to create the stars.

An interested Hen and a displaying Tom Turkey, *Meleagris gallopavo.*   Craig Tooley

Male Turkeys begin their mating dance too, displaying their magnificent tail feathers.

Wildlife Encounter with Tom Turkeys:

Andy Moore was watching a group of Tom Turkeys at The Sea Ranch. Andy has an iPhone with an unusual app, an app of turkey calls. He played the adult Hen call. All of the Toms came to an abrupt stop, turned around and headed toward Andy. They started displaying with their tail feathers and gobbling.

Andy remarked, "*I never thought I'd use my phone to talk to animals!*"

This is usually the month that Point Arena's most famous visitor leaves. Yes, Al, the Laysan Albatross, leaves for the seas south of the Aleutian Islands. We hope he - or she - will return in the late fall to grace us again with his or her presence.

Al, the Laysan Albatross, *Phoebastria immutabilis*, taking flight.   Craig Tooley

18

In March there is usually catch and release fishing for Steelhead on the Gualala and Garcia Rivers.

March Kayak Trip on the Gualala River:

" *I just took a twenty mile kayak trip with Chris Poehlmann and guests from Switzerland, starting from Clark's Crossing at Skagg's Springs Road. Pretty spectacular! There were actually some rapids at one spot, and some pretty choppy chutes and twists, but mostly beautiful swift currents.*

" *We saw one River Otter family and about thirty Mergansers – that's a lot of fish-eating. Only one big fish sighting: in a quiet eddy below the rapids, a very large fish – must have been a Steelhead – breached and slapped the water.*

" *Willow and Alder stabilized bars are trapping a lot of gravel, sand and silt just about everywhere, very positive indicators of the recovery of the river. Now all we need is for ocean conditions and river flows to allow for Steelhead and Coho to build back up. We hauled out at Mill Bend.*

" *We were the only kayak/canoe craft out there. It was more spectacular than a National Park, but without all the people!*"

—Peter Baye, Annapolis

Mark DeShields on the Gualala River with a beautiful Steelhead, *Oncorhynchus mykiss*, which he caught and then released. This fish had already spawned and was headed back to the ocean.   Jack Likins

The Gualala River at dusk.   Craig Tooley

Brant, *Branta bernicla*, flying low over the Pacific Ocean on their journey northward to their breeding grounds.

Craig Tooley

Brant, small black and white Geese, are seen migrating north. Flocks of a hundred or more can be seen streaming by in loose V formations along the Mendonoma Coast, undulating like a ribbon in the sky.

Aleutian Cackling Geese, formerly considered a small form of Canada Geese, are also seen in large flocks headed north with the imperative to create new life. They will stop on the coast of Humboldt and Del Norte counties to fatten up for their non-stop flight to islands in the Aleutians.

Male American Goldfinch, *Spinus tristis*, in breeding plumage. Craig Tooley

As the Brant and Aleutian Cackling Geese travel north, Swallows arrive, as do the bright-yellow male American Goldfinches. The females will follow in a few weeks. Putting up a thistle feeder often lures Goldfinches close to your home.

Daffodils, *Narcissus*, in Point Arena.   Craig Tooley

Residents and merchants of Point Arena have planted thousands of Daffodil bulbs and this is the month they bloom. This tiny city holds a big celebration on the second weekend in March – the Flower Power Festival and Daffodil Explosion.

Besides the beautiful flowers, the Point Arena Lighthouse awaits. It's a perfect place to spot whales and other wildlife.

Close by the Lighthouse is the Point Arena - Stornetta Public Lands, a wonderful place to hike and to see wildlife.

The Point Arena Lighthouse as seen from the air.

Craig Tooley

Al, the Albatross, Tundra Swans, and a Bald Eagle Sighting:

"*My husband and I had the treat of seeing Al the Albatross at Point Arena. While we were there we struck up a conversation with some birders, who told us about a flock of Tundra Swans on the Stornetta Lands.*

"*We drove to the area just north of the Point Arena Lighthouse to go for a hike, found the Tundra Swans, but to our even greater surprise and delight, also saw a Bald Eagle.*

"*We thought he was part of a piling at first – until he took flight. As he soared over the marshland, hundreds of birds scattered in different directions, apparently intent on not being his lunch.*

"*The only ones that were unmoved were the Tundra Swans, who swam placidly around, wondering what all the fuss was about.*" — Maureen Simons, The Sea Ranch

23

Craig Tooley photographed this immature Bald Eagle, *Haliaeetus leucocephalus*, in March.

It is uncommon to see a Bald Eagle, though sightings of this regal bird have increased recently, giving us hope that a pair will nest along the Mendonoma Coast.

Golden Eagles are also rarely seen. Hopefully one day soon these birds will be a common sighting. One was seen in Point Arena in March.

Wildlife Encounter with a Golden Eagle:

" *Richey Wasserman and I saw a Golden Eagle at least three times, most recently at the top of the big Cypress Trees across Lake Street from the high school. My wife, Madeline, and I were so enthralled staring at it through binoculars and getting out the bird book to be sure we were, in fact, viewing a Golden Eagle, that we didn't get a picture.*"

—Mitch McFarland, Point Arena

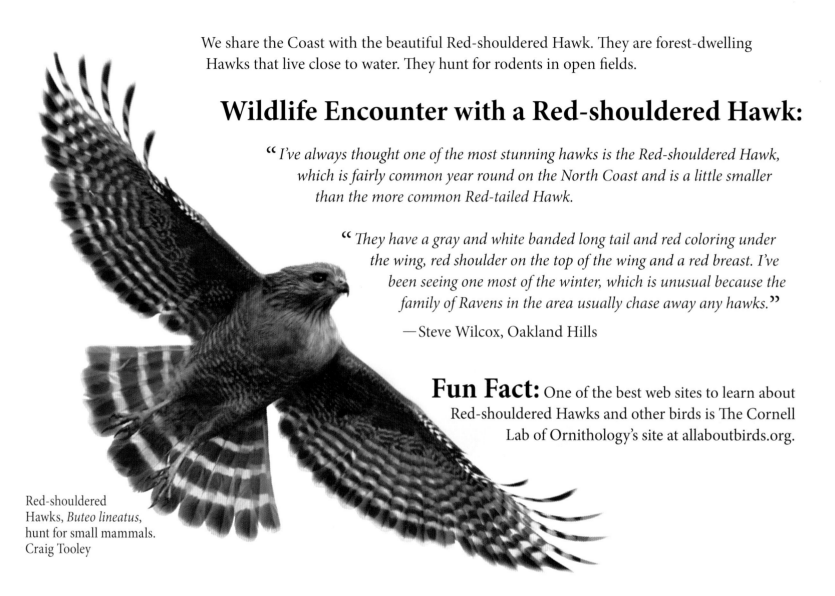

We share the Coast with the beautiful Red-shouldered Hawk. They are forest-dwelling Hawks that live close to water. They hunt for rodents in open fields.

Wildlife Encounter with a Red-shouldered Hawk:

" *I've always thought one of the most stunning hawks is the Red-shouldered Hawk, which is fairly common year round on the North Coast and is a little smaller than the more common Red-tailed Hawk.*

" *They have a gray and white banded long tail and red coloring under the wing, red shoulder on the top of the wing and a red breast. I've been seeing one most of the winter, which is unusual because the family of Ravens in the area usually chase away any hawks.* "

—Steve Wilcox, Oakland Hills

Fun Fact: One of the best web sites to learn about Red-shouldered Hawks and other birds is The Cornell Lab of Ornithology's site at allaboutbirds.org.

Red-shouldered Hawks, *Buteo lineatus*, hunt for small mammals. Craig Tooley

Bobcat, *Lynx rufus*, in a meadow.   Craig Tooley

Bobcats are year round residents of the Coast and can be seen in the daytime hunting rodents in grassy meadows.

Wildlife Encounter with a Bobcat:

" *We have an Iversen Lane resident Bobcat. She's been a good gopher catcher. Last year she arrived with a kitten and taught it to hunt while we were watching. She's beautiful and looks a light gray when it's raining.* "

— Doris Causey, Gualala

When the sky is clear, the stars are amazingly bright in March. The Coast's lack of light pollution is something to be cherished.

Appreciating the Late Night Sky:

"*I thought I was in a sea of stars. The sky was incredible and my first impulse was to call everyone I know and say, 'Look at the sky!' It was one of those nights clear as a bell. The constellations all ran into one another. It was so beautiful.*"

—Joann Harris, Anchor Bay

Moon and stars over the Pacific.   Craig Tooley

Spring arrives in late March. Celebrate the vernal equinox by renewing your relationship with Mother Nature and all the creatures that share this beautiful part of the world with us.

Osprey, *Pandion haliaetus*, laying the cornerstone to a new nest.   Drew Fagan

Mendonoma Sightings Throughout The Year

There is something special about spring rain when it is followed by a warm day. It seems as if you can see plants growing right in front of your eyes. Along with this burst of energy comes the process of creating new life. Birds can be seen with twigs in their beaks, building a nest in a secret location. Gray Foxes, Bobcats, and all our wildlife join in the cycle of life. Love, big time, is in the air. It's spring and the Mendonoma Coast beckons. Heed the call.

April is when Ospreys pair up and build, or rebuild, nests.

Fun Fact: Ospreys are
one of the largest birds of prey in North America with a wingspan up to six feet. Look for Ospreys fishing in the Coast's rivers and in the ocean. Any blufftop or beach could be a perfect spot to see an Osprey glide by.

Another Fun Fact:
An Osprey's eyesight is eight times sharper than that of a human.

Osprey, *Pandion haliaetus*, has piercing yellow eyes.   Craig Tooley

Ospreys are also called Sea Hawks or Fish Hawks, as they mostly hunt for fish. They will reuse a nest, year after year, laying two to four eggs each time. A nest in Anchor Bay has been used for over twenty consecutive years.

Excitement is in the air as April is the traditional start of the Abalone diving season. Richard Lewis put it like this, *"I am looking forward to the ocean laid out flat, like a lizard drinking."* Ten+ inch Abalones have been found this month.

Wildlife Encounter with Abalone:

" *We'd been in the water over two hours. We were diving at one of our favorite spots at The Sea Ranch. I found a ten-inch ab but while trying to measure it with my 10″ gauge I touched it and it clamped down on the rock so hard that I could not get it off.*

"*I called Ken over, he being stronger than me. He went down and, with all the strength he could muster, got it off of the rock. So technically it was his Abalone. The weirdest thing was that after bringing the Abalone to the surface, he dropped my iron back to the bottom (it was attached to a 40' float line), and when I went back down to look around, the iron was lying right next to another 10″ Abalone.*

"*It was a lucky day, but as I always say, 'It's amazing how lucky you are when you work hard at something.'* "

— Jack Likins, Gualala

Jack Likins and Ken Bailey with three ten-inch Abalones, *Haliotis rufescens*.   Richard Lewis

Local divers, like Jack and Ken, know to stay out of the water if conditions warrant it. Visitors, at their peril, aren't always willing to delay their dive. Give the Pacific Ocean all the respect she deserves.

Gray Whale, *Eschrichtius robustus*, mother and her calf.

Craig Tooley

April is a good month for spotting Gray Whale moms with their calves headed north to their feeding grounds in the Bering Sea.

Wildlife Encounter with Gray Whales:

Maureen Forys had two friends visiting at her Gualala cabin, one of whom faced a serious surgery.

"*Neither had ever spent much time in the area and I told them one of the great things about Gualala is that, if we were lucky, we might see some whales go by. And how Nature did deliver.*

"*Our first sighting was right at the mouth of the Gualala River. We spied a juvenile Gray Whale and two Dolphins feeding super close to the sandbar and the river breach. It was amazing! We could see barnacles on its back from shore. Then as we were looking out towards the horizon, we saw spout after spout heading north.*

"*Later that day we headed up to Point Arena for a drink at the pier, and the whales were still out in force. We saw dozens upon dozens of spouts as the whales came around the point. It was so special, exciting and heartening to see these gentle giants in such large numbers. My friend was calm and strong and felt that it was a good sign that everything will go well with her surgery and recovery. What a special place we live in with so much nature to enjoy and respect.*"
— Maureen Forys, Gualala

31

Harbor Seal pups begin birthing at the mouth of the Russian River, at Tide Pool Beach and Green Cove Rookeries on The Sea Ranch, and at other secluded coves on the Coast. The Sea Ranch has a wonderful docent program to inform visitors and locals about what they are seeing, while making sure people and their dogs stay away from the vulnerable pups.

Wildlife Encounter with a Harbor Seal Pup:

Irene Leidner came across a lone pup on Bowling Ball Beach.

"*It was a beautiful day and we saw a pup on the beach. We kept ourselves – and the three dogs with us – away from the pup, but called the Marin Rescue Center when we returned home. According to the volunteer we spoke with, pups are left to fend for themselves around this time of year. We hope everything was okay, especially because our eight-year-old granddaughter was so concerned.*"

Newborn Harbor Seal pup, *Phoca vitulina.*   Craig Tooley

Never "rescue" one of these pups. The mothers leave them alone on the beach while they fish to feed themselves. These pups are not abandoned; the mothers will return to nurse their sweet pups. If you do see a pup or any other marine mammal in distress, call the Marine Mammal Center at (415) 289-SEAL [(415) 289-7325]. They will assign a local volunteer to come and assess the situation.

Sierran Treefrogs, also called Pacific Chorus Frogs, begin calling to attract a mate. For such a tiny frog they can really make a big sound. This is the frog that produces the classic "ribbit, ribbit" call.

Fun Fact: Only the males have this vocal sac. When it is not extended, as it is in this photo, it looks like a dark patch on the frog's throat.

Another Fun Fact: This frog can change its color to adapt to its environment.

Sierran Treefrog, *Pseudacris sierra*, in full throat. Peter Baye

The Sierran Treefrog, *Pseudacris sierra*, has toe pads that allow it to climb easily. Craig Tooley

Pacific Wren, *Troglodytes pacificus*, formerly called Winter Wren, sings.   Craig Tooley

As you listen for the call of the Sierran Treefrog, you can also listen for a male Pacific Wren singing its "rush-for-words" love song. One was heard near Salal Creek on The Sea Ranch. Another was heard in a forest in Anchor Bay.

The trail along Salal Creek is a public access trail. You will find the trailhead near the entrance to Gualala Point Regional Park. After you pass through the pay station, enter the parking area to the left. On your left you will see the first signs marking this trail. There is a beautiful waterfall to discover if we've had enough rain.

Another bird to listen for is the returning Swainson's Thrush. It has the most beautiful song, with flute-like trills going higher and higher. Hearing this Thrush singing at the first hint of dawn signifies Spring.

Salal Creek's hidden waterfall.   Craig Tooley

April brings the great Loon migration. Thousands upon thousands fly by, mostly Pacific Loons but some Common and Red-throated Loons too. They come in waves of ten to a hundred or more, flying just off the bluffs. The increasing sunlight has told them it's time to return to their breeding grounds to the north.

Pacific Loons, *Gavia pacifica*, migrating north.   Craig Tooley

Wildlife Encounter with Loons:

"*I noticed a lot of Pacific Loons going by. So I decided to try and get some kind of an accurate number by counting them for 10 minutes and using the equation: (L/10) x 60 minutes x 24 hours = Total Pacific Loons in one day, where L is the number of Pacific Loons observed in a 10-minute interval.*

"*After eating a bag of peanuts I came up with the following data. One whale, probably a Gray, and a count of 16.25 Pacific Loons per minute, which gives us 975 Loons in an hour or 23,400 Pacific Loons a day. Thatsa lotta Loons.*"

— The Loon Ranger, Mendocino Headlands.

Coveys of California Quail thrive where there is underbrush for them to hide from predators. Unfortunately their main predator is the oh-so-common house cat.

California Quail, *Callipepla californica*, are sociable birds that often gather in groups called coveys.   Craig Tooley

A Mysterious Wildlife Encounter with California Quail:

"*I looked out my window to enjoy our local covey of Quail. There were fourteen, and I could tell that for sure because they were not moving.*

"*Wait a minute! When is the last time you saw Quail that were not in constant motion? It was as if someone hit the 'pause' button on a movie, and I started to wonder if it was me? No…the waves were still moving, and the leaves were still swaying in the breeze. Fascinated, I watched and waited for them to move.*

"*Some had their beaks on the ground, one was turning to look over his wing, others were frozen looking at each other, or bushes or like the game of 'statues' we used to play as kids. One minute went by, and then two. Then 'pop' one twitched and they all scooted off into the bushes. What was going on?*" — Dale Phelps, Gualala

There was danger nearby, possibly a Hawk, and the Quail froze in an attempt to blend into their surroundings. It must have seemed like the Twilight Zone!

Male American Goldfinch, *Carduelis tristis*, in breeding plumage.   Craig Tooley

Wildlife Encounter with American Goldfinches:

"*I enjoy them so much. In spring I tie skeins of raw wool to various trees and it is the Goldfinches who visit these the most for nest building materials. They always come as a pair with the male on a higher branch to keep watch over the female as she 'shops.'*

"*Some are very picky about which small hair they will pull from the fleece. We love to watch them select one hair, stretch to pull it loose and then stuff it into their mouths to add the sticky saliva.*"

— Jane Reichhold, Gualala

Birds of all kinds are building nests, some with mud, some with twigs, some with grasses and some with yarn. Violet-green Swallows and Western Bluebirds are nesting in cavities of snags or custom-built birdhouses. Hummingbirds use spider webs as the main ingredient in their nests. That's a good enough reason to leave spider webs alone.

Great Egret, *Ardea alba*, with nesting materials. Craig Tooley

White-crowned Sparrow, *Zonotrichia leucophrys*, with nesting materials, sitting on Lupine. Craig Tooley

Fence Lizards, Alligator Lizards and Western Skinks burst into activity during the mild April weather.

A juvenile Western Skink, *Eumeces skiltonianus*, a small lizard that loves to bask in the sun.

Peter Baye

While Bobcats are year round residents, April is when adults begin hunting for their young. Bobcats have been spotted this month north of Point Arena; one was seen crossing Lighthouse Road. And the meadows at Manchester and The Sea Ranch are prime spots to see one.

Fun Fact: Bobcats can live to twenty-three years and are often seen hunting small mammals in meadows.

Bobcats, *Lynx rufus*, have tufted ears.

Craig Tooley

Wildlife Encounter with Brown Pelicans:

Our beloved Brown Pelicans return to the Mendonoma Coast on their post-breeding dispersal from Baja California. It's a welcome sight to see them glide by.

"*Today I saw the first Brown Pelicans cross my view. They were in the classic V formation. I stand, look, and feel my heart within actually pause – a stunning moment.*" — Tom Eckles, Gualala

Brown Pelican, *Pelecanus occidentalis*, over the beautiful Pacific Ocean.

Craig Tooley

California Huckleberry, *Vaccinium ovatum*.   Craig Tooley
Its blossoms turn into dark blue or black berries in the summer.

Hoverfly, *Syrphidae*, feeding on Wild Lilac, *Ceanothus*.   Craig Tooley

Many wildflowers begin blooming this month. California Mustard begins its riotious bloom. Huckleberry bushes are loaded with white and pink blossoms, letting us know good things are to come when the berries ripen in summer.

Coastal Fairy Bells shyly hide their exquisite, bell-shaped blooms under their leaves. A few Pacific Rhododendrons begin their bloom joined by Lupines, False Solomon Seals, Dogtooth Violets, Wild Lilac, Star-Lilies, Yellow Monkey Flower, Redwood Violets, fragrant Western Azaleas and Fritillary. They join many other wildflowers in ushering in Spring.

Along with the blooms come our native bees. Bumblebees can be seen feeding on Wild Lilac. Native bees are busy working Huckleberry and Manzanita blossoms, doing the job assigned to them by Mother Nature. Joining the Bees in pollinating flowers are Hoverflies.

Fun Fact: There are nearly one thousand species of native Bees in California. Twenty-six are Bumblebees. Our vital native Bees pollinate our native plants. Yellow Jackets can be pests at an outdoor picnic, however they also have their role to play in nature, pollinating many flowers. Hoverflies are also called Syrhid Flies. They too are pollinators. Along with feeding on nectar, they eat aphids.

Indian Warriors bloom in April. The roots of this plant often attach themselves to other plants, especially Manzanita, to obtain nutrients. As is the case with most of our native wildflowers, this plant has medicinal qualities. It also has a legend – that each of these striking plants grows for a fallen warrior.

Indian Warriors, *Pedicularis densiflora*, are parasitic plants.   Craig Tooley

A walk on a coastal bluff offers a veritable feast for the eyes as wildflowers spring up. Baby Blue Eyes are one of the standouts you might seek. The bluffs at Salt Point State Park, Manchester Beach, at Hearn Gulch, and at Black Point on The Sea Ranch would all be good places to see them. Dogwoods are blooming in a blinding array of white flowers in Annapolis.

Wildflowers at Salt Point State Park.

Craig Tooley

And then there's the aptly named Witch's Teeth, a tiny wildflower that blooms in April.

Witch's Teeth, *Lotus formosissimus*, is a member of the Pea family.   Craig Tooley

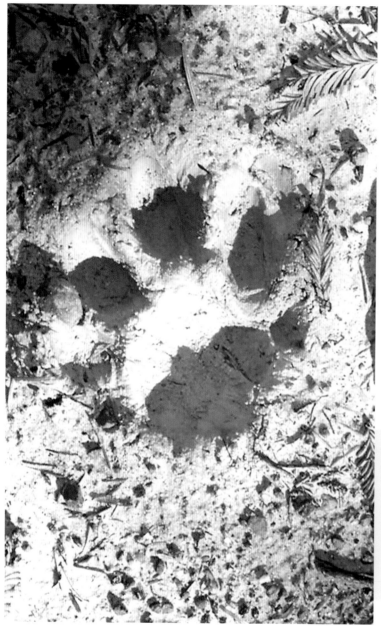

Mountain Lion, *Puma concolor*, paw print – notice there are no claw marks, as the big cat's claws are recessed when walking.

Eric G. Anderson

Mountain Lions, though a rare sighting, have been seen this month – at The Sea Ranch, north of Anchor Bay near Schooner Gulch, and by Windy Hollow Road in Point Arena.

Wildlife Encounter with a Mountain Lion:

Annie Beckett and her husband, Jerry Immel, had just turned onto Leeward in The Sea Ranch at 10:04 p.m.

"*A truly enormous Mountain Lion trotted at a leisurely pace across our car's path. It was larger than a full-grown Great Dane, with a tail longer than its back legs, probably three inches in diameter! Jerry estimates its weight at about 180 pounds. It moved across the road, around the corner of a house and off out of sight. One impressive cat.*"

— Annie Beckett, The Sea Ranch

Fun Facts: Male Mountain Lions can weigh between 180 and 300 pounds. Their length, from nose to tail tip, can be eight feet, with the tail making up about one-third of the total. Females are smaller. They hunt Deer and smaller mammals, like Coyotes and Raccoons. They are also called Cougars or Pumas and can live for about twelve years in the wild.

Lambs and Kids continue to be born in the grazing herd on The Sea Ranch, each adding greatly to the cuteness factor of the Coast.

FUN FACT:

The Sea Ranch flock of Sheep and Goats is an ecological way to keep the grasses mowed, thus lowering the fire danger. There are about 350 members in the herd and they are thriving. You can find out where they are grazing at this website: thesearanchsheep.com.

Inquisitive Lamb, *Ovis aries.*

Craig Tooley

North American River Otters can give birth in April. These sleek creatures are very susceptible to pollution. It's heartening to see them thrive near creeks and rivers on the Mendonoma Coast. Look for them near the mouth of the Gualala River from the Gualala Bluff Trail, at Salal Creek on The Sea Ranch, off the Point Arena Pier and at other waterways of the Coast.

Wildlife Encounter with River Otters:

"*While standing on the dock at Point Arena I saw a large Otter foraging around the rocks about 100 yards out in the water. After about five minutes it swam to the shore, got out of the water and hustled around the edge of the shore rocks. Then it went back in and swam directly under me standing on the dock. I'm wondering if it was a Sea Otter.*"

—Steve Padula, Gualala

Female River Otter, *Lontra canadensis*, with her pups.
Craig Tooley

Fun Fact: One difference between River Otters and Sea Otters is that Sea Otters spend their lives at sea. Sea Otters swim on their backs and are found far to our south. River Otters are able to come on land and swim in the sea. And they swim with their tummies down.

Experiencing The Pacific Ocean:

Spring brings windy weather, especially in the afternoons. But sometimes the north-west wind takes a day off, leaving the ocean like a lake.

"*With the ocean looking remarkably like Lake Tahoe, I took my boat out to a spot below Moat Creek to go for a swim. Anchoring in a small, secluded cove, I felt like I had the ocean all to myself.*

"*Slipping over the side I was met with clouds of krill and 30 feet of visibility. I found a small chute at about 20 feet and hid between two boulders to watch the show. A parade of blue and black Rockfish soon appeared, quickly followed by a Lingcod on the prowl. A timid – or very smart – black and yellow Rockfish cowered nervously on the bottom.*

"*Rising to the surface to take a breath, I was greeted with beautiful sunshine and calm water. How many times have I wished for calm seas, only to be met with 20-knot winds and 10-foot breaking swells? Living in paradise, when the ocean opens her arms and invites us in, we need to drop everything and go.*" —Bob LaMar, Point Arena

A calm day at Cook's Beach.

Craig Tooley

49

Bald Eagles have been spotted in April. Two were seen in Albion, several in Jenner, and one flying by with a fish in its talons at Ocean Cove Campground near Timber Cove.

It's a treat to hear Owls calling in the night. One species we hear is the Western Screech Owl. And, wouldn't you know it – this Owl doesn't screech; it has a lilting call.

Western Screech Owl, *Megascops kennicottii.*   Ron LeValley

Wildlife Encounter with a Western Screech Owl:

Angela Ferrari was in a back room at her house in Point Arena when she heard a thud on her window. Her kitty, Lucy, looked at her with eyes wide. Angela went outside and found the Owl still breathing.

She carefully cradled it and took it to her garage. As it recovered it flew up into the rafters. Angela called a friend to help her release the Owl. He managed to get the Owl down. It clung to his finger and finally flew away.

Then a month later Angela had her doors and windows open. The Screech Owl returned, flew into her kitchen and perched on the pot rack above her stove. As it stared at her Angela said, "*You're back. So nice to see you!*" After a while Angela picked it up. "*It let me! It was most handsome. I took it outside and tossed it into the air.*"

It seemed to Angela that it returned to thank her for her care - a magical experience.

Spotted Owls are an exceptional sighting. They need old-growth forests to nest.

Fun Fact:
Spotted Owls eat small mammals, especially Wood Rats.

Not So Fun Fact:
Due to habitat loss this Owl is considered threatened.

A juvenile Spotted Owl, *Strix occidentalis*, perhaps six to eight weeks old.

Craig Tooley

The male cones of Bishop Pine Trees release yellow pollen this month, coating cars and causing distress for those with allergies. If you dare, swing a branch and watch the yellow cloud erupt. Douglas-fir limbs are tipped with light green growth, bringing fanciful thoughts of nail polish.

A Rainbow Experience:

Liz Redfield was working at the Gualala Arts Center. She wrote,

"*It was magical. I looked up from the desk and out the window to see the sun shining, yet the rain was pouring down.*

"*I thought there must be a rainbow, so I went outside to find the rainbow's end was right before me from the ground up through the Redwood Trees lining the new Deprima Terrace. Was I in a dream? How lucky I was to experience this, like nothing I've ever experienced before!*"

Fun Fact:
April showers bring vibrant rainbows to the Mendonoma Coast.

Rainbow north of Fish Rocks.   Jeanne Jackson

There can be new life in April at the B. Bryan Preserve in Point Arena, a wildlife sanctuary. A newborn Grevy's Zebra is surprised at its first glimpse of a Gopher.

Fun Fact: Grevy's Zebras are native to eastern Africa. Dr. Frank Mello and Judy Mello of the B. Bryan Preserve are working to breed and study these extremely endangered creatures. Grevy's Zebras in Point Arena? You bet!

Newborn Grevy's Zebra, *Equus grevyi.*
"Mom, what the heck did I just see?"

Craig Tooley

Gray Foxes delight us with their antics and they are proficient rodent hunters. Those plagued with Gophers are happy to see them at work.

Wildlife Encounter with a Gray Fox:

" *For weeks we've been amazed how quickly our two Hummingbird feeders – each about five feet from the ground – were emptying. Hungry birds, we thought. Then yesterday we noticed our resident Gray Fox had climbed up the entry bench structure and was helping himself.* " — Maynard and Lu Lyndon, The Sea Ranch.

Gray Fox, *Urocyon cinereoargenteus*, relaxes on a Redwood stump.

Craig Tooley

It seems like every creature on the Coast is smiling in April.

Smiling Pocket Gopher, *Geomyidae*.

Allen Vinson

Never lose your wonder of our natural world. In that way you'll be forever young.
Enjoy the magic of spring on the Coast as it captures your senses and brings you joy.

Pale Swallowtail Butterfly, *Papilio eurymedon*, feeding on a thistle.

Craig Tooley

Mendonoma Sightings Throughout The Year

Whether you are looking down for wildflowers, looking out over the ocean for Whales and Dolphins, or looking up to see what is winging through the air, you are bound to see something beautiful in May.

Jeanne's Wildlife Encounter:

"*While enjoying the warm spring weather, Osprey calls filled the air. Two, then three and finally four Ospreys were wheeling in the oh-so-blue sky. A lovely Swallowtail Butterfly landed on a nearby flower.*

"*When the Ospreys departed, the musical trills of American Goldfinches and Pine Siskins were heard, along with the brash counterpoint of several Acorn Woodpeckers.*

"*It was a feast for anyone willing to slow down, look and listen. And with those sightings came a sense of wonder and a profound gratitude for being here on the Mendonoma Coast.*"

By the beginning of May, and often just in time for Mother's Day, Fawns make their beautiful wobbly-legged appearance. This is the time of year to be especially careful driving on the Coast. If you see a Doe cross the highway or a road, put on your flashing lights, and wait a minute in case a Fawn or two or even three are close behind. Create a Mendonoma traffic jam – two cars, perhaps. Your reward for waiting a moment might be the sighting of pure loveliness.

Wildlife Encounter with Newborn Fawns:

" *I saw my first young Fawns. I was driving by the golf course on Sea Ranch and a Doe appeared beside me. She had a pair of twins with legs that were a bit unsteady. One came right up to my stopped vehicle for a sniff! Mama said something discrete and they all scampered away.* "

— Clay Yale, The Sea Ranch

A newborn Fawn, *Odocoileus hemionus columbianus.*   Craig Tooley

White Fawn, *Odocoileus hemionus columbianus*, coloring up.   Craig Tooley

Fun Fact:

In 2006, 2009 and 2013 the Mendonoma Coast has had a white Fawn born. They are considered towheads. They managed to survive their original lack of camouflage and eventually did color up.

Female Osprey, *Pandion haliaetus*, and her chick watch as the male brings dinner.

Paul Brewer

Male Ospreys are fishing for their mates who are tending the nest. Hatchlings may be born in May and the feeding frenzy will intensify.

Fun Fact: The female Osprey is larger than the male and sits on the nest. The male brings her and the chick all kinds of fish. The adults will briefly exchange places on the nest so she can perch nearby and eat.

Wildlife Encounter with an Osprey and an Eel:

Willie Brown was traveling down Highway One near Glennen Drive in Gualala when he saw an Osprey with an Eel in its talons. He said the bird was struggling mightily and was barely able to fly above the phone line but it prevailed.

It's amazing what you see when you give yourself the gift of time. What could be more precious in this busy world of ours?

Harbor Seal pups continue to be born in secluded coves, though pups born earlier are being weaned from their mother's milk. Those pups aren't happy about it and lots of complaining can be heard emanating from the coves. However, Harbor Seal pups and their moms have a close and loving relationship.

Harbor Seal Pup, *Phoca vitulina*, nuzzling its mom.   Craig Tooley

In the spring it is wise to plan your bluff-top or beach adventures for the morning hours as the afternoon brings the ubiquitous northwest winds. These winds produce the necessary upwelling of nutrients in the Pacific Ocean to feed surface fish and other organisms. The waters off the Mendonoma Coast are rich in these nutrients – a fortune beyond compare.

The Pacific Ocean, whose murmuring underscores our daily lives, sometimes gives a careful watcher a priceless gift. A pair of Orcas has been spotted off Anchor Bay in May. A Humpback has been seen cruising the kelp forest south of Del Mar Point on The Sea Ranch. Gray Whales, mothers with their calves, continue to be seen, migrating northward.

Wildlife Encounter with Gray Whales and a Tag-Along Minke Whale:

Linda Morley-Wells had been enjoying watching many Brown Pelicans and Loons flying north, along with migrating Gray Whales.

" *Walt and I saw groups of Gray Whales migrating north, some so close to shore that the waves were breaking on* *top of them. We saw a Minke Whale traveling with a group of Grays for protection. It could be indicative of the arrival of Orcas who return to our coast at the time the young Harbor Seals go out to sea.*

" *Nature is always busy on the Coast.* "

And Harbor Porpoises have been spotted this month, slicing through calm waters.

Fun Fact: You can identify Harbor Porpoises by their small triangular black fins. They are not commonly found near shore and are best seen on flat, calm days.

Not So Fun Fact: The number of Harbor Porpoises is declining. Because of their feeding habits, they are often caught in gill nets set on the bottom of the ocean. These gill nets act like a curtain in the sea, inadvertently drowning these beautiful animals.

Harbor Porpoises, *Phocoena phocoena*, off The Sea Ranch.

Craig Tooley

Some Huckleberry bushes are beginning to set fruit with great masses of little green berries soon to ripen in the months to come. Others are still dotted with tiny white and pink blossoms.

Fun Fact: If you note which Huckleberry bushes are loaded with blossoms now, it will be easier to find the ripe berries in the summer. Not all Huckleberry bushes bear fruit every year.

The Bush Monkey-flower blooms in sunny spots. A California native, it requires no summer water. Hummingbirds appreciate its abundant blossoms. It has medicinal qualities and it's a host plant for the Checkerspot Butterfly.

Fun Fact: This plant is also called Sticky Monkey Flower. It has antiseptic qualities. Pomo and Miwok peoples used its flowers and roots to help heal scrapes and burns.

Bush Monkey-flowers, *Mimulus aurantiacus*, are rich in nectar.   Craig Tooley

Alum-Root, with its tiny white flowers that look like little stars, begins blooming on the forest floor. Native peoples knew it for its powerful medicinal qualities, including as an astringent and an antiseptic. The leaves carpet the forest long before the slender flower stalk appears.

Alum-Root, *Heuchera*, is often found on the forest floor.

Craig Tooley

Pacific Rhododendrons, more commonly called Wild Rhododendrons, come into their full beauty in May. You can see them blooming along Highway 1 at Salt Point State Park or at Kruse Rhododendron State Reserve on Kruse Ranch Road.

Visit the Mendocino Coast Botanical Gardens in Fort Bragg this month for a very special reward – multitudes of Rhododendrons in bloom. And if you take the trail all the way to the bluff, you'll find a wonderful spot to whale watch.

Pacific Rhododendron, *Rhododendron macrophyllum*.   Craig Tooley

Five miles south of the Botanical Gardens in Fort Bragg is the fascinating Jug Handle State Natural Reserve. There is an ecological staircase to be discovered. The nature trail takes you up through several terraces, each 100,000 years older than the previous one, ending at a pygmy forest.

Fun Fact: The Pomo people used Rhododendron blossoms to create wreaths which were used in dances, in particular for their Strawberry Festivals.

Wild Azaleas are near peak bloom, though their blooms will continue into the summer. Some are quite fragrant so do yourself a favor and take a deep breath when you are close by a blossom.

Western Azaleas, *Rhododendron occidentale*, are found in moist areas on the Mendonoma Coast.

Craig Tooley

Jeanne's Encounter with Wildflowers:

"*Ralph Waldo Emerson once wrote, 'The Earth laughs in flowers.' As the spring wildflower show continues to delight, I fancy that I can hear Mother Earth giggle when I see a coastal bluff of tiny wildflowers, hunkered down against the afternoon breezes. The sighting of the first Wild Azaleas brings the sound of a bubbling chortle. And when the forest is brightened by the splashy Clintonias, I can hear her laugh out loud.*

"*Listen and perhaps you will hear it too.*"

Another native wildflower that shines in May is the magnificent Clintonia, also called Andrew's Clintonia. A member of the Lily family, it blooms in the shade of the forest.

Fun Fact: Clintonias are also called Blue Bead Lilies for the cobalt-blue berries they sport later in the summer.

Andrew's Cintonia, *Clintonia andrewsiana*, is a dramatic wildflower found in mixed forests on the Coast.

Craig Tooley

Northern Alligator Lizards have been seen mating in May. It's a startling sight as the male appears to be biting the head or neck of the female.

Love bites – Northern Alligator Lizards, *Elgaria coerulea*, mating.

Craig Tooley

Raccoons are incredibly intelligent creatures. Their facial markings are one of the reasons why they are called "masked bandits."

Wildlife Encounter with a Raccoon Wanna-Be Thief:

Art Thompson was all set for a nice day on The Sea Ranch golf links. He leaned his golf bag outside the pro shop and went inside. He glanced back at his bag only to see a very brazen Raccoon approaching. Before Art could react, the Raccoon ripped a pocket right out of the bag.

Art chased it away before the thief got to Art's stash of a banana and some peanuts. You know you should never turn your back on the ocean. Now you know you should never turn your back on your golf bag!

Raccoon, *Procyon lotor*, mom with two little masked bandits.

Craig Tooley

Black Bears have been sighted this month on The Sea Ranch, in Annapolis and in Anchor Bay. Bears are a natural part of the Coast and occasionally ramble through. Residents have learned to secure their garbage and not to leave any pet food outside. It's always a good idea to keep our wildlife wild.

Two Bald Eagles have been seen near the Ledford House on Spring Grove Road in Albion in May.

Bald Eagle, *Haliaeetus leucocephalus*.

Paul Brewer

Wildlife Encounter with Bald Eagles:

"*A huge bird came over the cliffs flying east toward the hills. I grabbed my binoculars and saw another bird. They were two Bald Eagles. I was able to observe them as they drifted over the hills between Salmon Creek and the Albion estuary.*

"*Seeing them together made me wonder if they might be a mated pair. Would it not be wonderful if we ended up with a resident pair? I would be thrilled.*"

— Chris Skyhawk, Albion

Brown Pelicans are migrating north in great numbers. There is something about Brown Pelicans that lifts the spirit. To see them in formation, doing a flyby, feels like a gift. They rest on offshore rocks and islands and can be seen plunge diving for food.

Wildlife Encounter with Brown Pelicans:

" *Many people I know – myself included – think of these birds as being almost mystical. The first sighting of the Pelicans in the spring is always so exciting and seeing them flying overhead or along-side you on the bluffs is magical.*

"*Sitting in a beach chair watching them 'hunt' as they dive into the water after fish is better than anything on TV.*"

—Wendy Bailey, Gualala

Brown Pelican, *Pelecanus occidentalis*, plunge diving for fish.   Craig Tooley

Abalone season continues in May when conditions permit. During a dive many wonders can be seen.

An Abalone Dive During a Rainstorm:

"*It was raining pretty hard. We had a great dive. Explored some new areas on the south side of where I like to dive at Arch Rock. We had at least 25 feet visibility.*

"*We saw lots of fish – schools of blacks, a couple of small lings, and one big cabezon, which would have made some really tasty fish tacos but I didn't bring a spear gun. There were lots of abalones two inches to four inches in shallow, and a very healthy population of abs up to 9 7/8 inches.*

"*This reef was really healthy – nudibranchs, sea urchins, green-lings, anemones, crabs, shrimp, scallops and sponges. I saw a 1.5 meter orange sponge under a ledge that had to be 75 years old at least! Everything was vibrant. We even had a huge bull Sea Lion swim with us for about 15 minutes.*"

—Ken Bailey, Gualala

Fun Fact: Sea Sponges have no brains or central nervous systems. They feed by filtering plankton and other nutrients received from ocean currents through their many pores.

An orange Sea Sponge, *Porifera*, an animal that lives on the ocean floor.   Ken Bailey

North American River Otter pups continue to be born in May. They seem to take great joy in being alive, playing with each other, swimming in the ocean and in rivers. They have been seen sliding down muddy riverbanks and on slippery kelp beds. Life can be good when you are a River Otter.

Wildlife Encounter with a River Otter Pup, a Warning and Good Advice:

" *We were called to Walk-On-Beach where a little River Otter pup was huddled under some logs in the sand, alone. Dogs had been harrying it. We left it hoping mom would come back.*

" *The next morning there were tracks leading up to a hidey-hole and the little squirt was gone. Mom and her other little ones probably were watching from cover all day, worrying. Please keep dogs on leashes and in control. If you find little 'abandoned' animals anywhere, back away quietly and let the moms find them.* "

—Sandy Bush,
The Sea Ranch/Lacey, WA.

River Otter pup, *Lontra canadensis*, playing on the rocks.   Craig Tooley

Bobcat, *Lynx rufus*, has a gopher in his sights.   Drew Fagan

A Bobcat has been observed chasing Wild Turkeys north of Point Arena, but mostly they hunt smaller mammals such as gophers and voles.

Bobcat cubs have been seen near Riverside Road in Point Arena in May.

Frogs deposit egg masses in tributaries of the Coast's rivers. The Foothill Yellow-legged Frog is native and declining in other areas but doing well in the Gualala River Watershed.

Wildlife Encounter with Frog Eggs:

"*It was heartening to see masses of Foothill Yellow-legged Frog eggs deposited in the stream bed of the North Fork of Fuller Creek. The masses are approximately four to six inches in diameter.*" —Lee Tate, Annapolis

Fun Fact: There's a web site to hear frog calls at amphibiaweb.org. A Western Toad has a call you would think came from a bird!

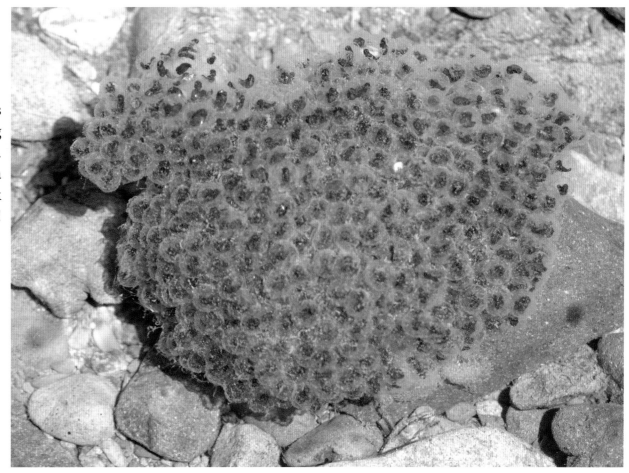

Egg mass of Foothill Yellow-legged Frog, *Rana boylii*.   Lee Tate and Darrell Paige

In the latter part of May the first fledgling birds are seen, particularly Dark-eyed Juncos and Steller's Jays. The babies will often flutter their wings and make a particular call to prompt their hardworking parents to place a seed or a bug in their mouths.

Young Oak Titmouse, *Baeolophus inornatus*, waiting to be fed.   Craig Tooley

And, to add to the wonders of May, Gray Fox kits begin to be born.

Our wildlife touches us on so many different levels and is so worthy of being treasured and protected. It is one of the reasons we love living here or visiting this beautiful part of the world.

Very young Gray Fox kit, *Urocyon cinereoargenteus*.   Craig Tooley

The early morning fog softens and
quiets the beginning of the day.
When the fog lifts, the Mendonoma
Coast is revealed, as if for the first time.
It is summer and the thrum of new life
is in the air. Leave your cares behind
and open your senses to this part
of the world we love so much.

Dawn on the Mendonoma Coast.

Craig Tooley

Mendonoma Sightings Throughout The Year

We have one constant that is so easy to take for granted. Sometimes murmuring, other times demanding to be heard, glistening in the afternoon sun – we are in awe of the mesmerizing Pacific Ocean.

June can bring the first heat wave of the year. With the fog swept away by the warm offshore breezes, the sunrises are spectacular – visions of pastel layered on pastel, a reward from Mother Nature for waking up early.

Our first heat wave is often followed by fog. Coastal fog is Mother Nature's air conditioning. Folks who live inland where it's hot often travel to the Coast for relief. When the sun breaks through, the ocean reveals its treasures to those fortunate enough to be in the right place at the right time.

Sea Stars, commonly called Starfish, can be seen at low tide on the big rocks.

A Sea Star, *Asteroidea*, party.

Craig Tooley

Fun Fact: Most Sea Stars have five arms, but some will have six or more.

Sunflower Sea Star, *Asteroidea*, with eighteen arms.

Craig Tooley

Salmon fishing can be good in June when the wind relents. In the evening you might see a necklace of lights formed by the fishing fleet at harbor off Anchor Bay, Point Arena and other safe spots. Fishermen will sometimes sell their catch at Noyo harbor in Fort Bragg, the Point Arena pier or in front of the Gualala Post Office. Your taste buds will dance for joy!

Along with the Salmon, Humpbacks and Orcas and Dolphins have been seen in June. Orcas have an erect, very tall black dorsal fin. A pod has been seen just north of the Point Arena Lighthouse.

Fun Fact: Orcas are also called Killer Whales even though they actually are Dolphins.

A pair of Orcas, *Orcinus orca*. Female Orcas have a smaller dorsal fin.

Tom Eckles

Risso's Dolphins – a pod of a hundred or more –
have been seen off the Little River Headlands.

Humpbacks are exciting to see as they seem to take great
joy in breaching.

Wildlife Encounter with Humpback Whales:

"*We have been observing Humpback Whales feeding but one evening was capped off with spectacular breaches. A pod of three began pursuing one another. The scenario was carried out repeatedly.*

"*Of the eight breaches, three were in tandem as though carried out by synchronized swimmers. The perfectly timed breaches produced a spectacular aquatic display of leviathan magnitude.*"

—Fred McElroy, Saunders Reef, Gualala

Humpback Whale, *Megaptera novaeangliae*, propelling itself out of the Pacific Ocean.

Craig Tooley

Sometimes the Pacific Ocean is so calm that a sea kayak adventure is possible. And that might bring you a sighting of curious California Sea Lions.

Wildlife Encounters at the Point Arena Lighthouse:

"*One of our summer gangs of Sea Lions is back. About thirty of them have taken up residence on the outer reef, basking, barking and burning off excess testosterone. Meanwhile, the resident Harbor Seals moved to rocks as far away from their boisterous cousins as possible and continue their silent sunning.*

"*We've enjoyed watching a flock of twenty to thirty Brown Pelicans repeatedly circle the point at around fifty feet. They seem to be playing a game of 'He Who Flaps First, Loses' as* they ride the air currents and updrafts of Point Arena. Seeing them through binoculars from the Lighthouse tower coming straight at you, one can't help thinking of a Blue Angels performance.*

"*While most visitors to the Lighthouse come for the spectacular views of the Coast and countryside, many leave talking about the amazing wildlife they've seen.*"

—Glenn Funk, Anchor Bay

Fun Fact: Sea Lions are very intelligent and playful. Most pups are born in June and July in southern California and Mexico. There is an active colony of male Sea Lions on Fish Rocks off Anchor Bay.

California Sea Lions, *Zalophus californianus*, off the Sonoma Coast, as seen from a kayak.
Craig Tooley

Plankton bloom usually begins in June. It can reduce visibility in the ocean to as little as three feet, making Abalone diving nearly impossible. The strong northwest winds of spring continue to upwell nutrient-rich water from the ocean floor near our shores. Along with the sun, the nutrients brought up can cause a phytoplankton bloom. Phytoplankton are microscopic marine plants. They are the basis of almost all ocean food webs. Krill and Jellyfish, among others, eat them.

Fun Fact: Jellyfish are found in all oceans and seas of Earth. They are beautiful creatures that come in an array of striking colors.

Not So Fun Fact: Their sting can be very painful and, in some cases, deadly. Look but don't touch is a good motto for Jellyfish.

Jellyfish, *Medusozoa*, look ethereal as they slowly pass by.   Craig Tooley

Leopard Lily, *Lilium pardalinum*, is also called Tiger Lily.   Craig Tooley

That splash of orange is a beautiful wildflower that blooms in June. It's called Leopard Lily or Tiger Lily because of the spots it displays. This lily is usually found near water and the flowers are on top of a two-to-three foot stem. Never pick them as the flower head develops a pod, which later in the summer will contain tiny brown seeds needed for its reproduction.

Fun Legend: If you smell a Tiger Lily, you are sure to get freckles.

Another wildflower to look for this month is the California Milkwort, which sports small, pinkish, pea-shaped flowers. It often is found blooming under Manzanita. Wild Stream Orchids can sometimes be found near Leopard Lilies. They grow in the bed and banks of bedrock-exposed reaches of the Gualala River.

Fun Fact: To learn more about the Gualala River go to the Friends of the Gualala River website at gualalariver.org.

Scarlet Monkeyflowers, not as common as the yellow ones, begin to bloom. Ithuriel's Spear can be seen blooming on grassy hillsides. Goldfields and California Poppies peak now. And Coast Lilies grace us with their short-lived beauty in June.

A Coast Lily, *Lilium maritimum*, unfurling.   Craig Tooley

Whether we live in, or briefly visit, such a beautiful part of the world, investing the time to watch, look, and listen pays back untold rewards.

And what could be more rewarding than seeing Gray Fox kits? Gray Foxes are year round residents of the Coast and they are raising their young in June. The mother nurses the tiny kits and the father is close by, on guard for any danger.

Wildlife Encounter with Gray Fox Kits:

" *We have four baby Fox kits whose parents made residence in our woodshed, just outside our bedroom window. They are darling! All have unique characteristic markings and personalities. Both male and female adults guard and care for them. It is an absolute joy to watch.*"

—Rita Peck, The Sea Ranch

Gray Fox kits, *Urocyon cinereoargenteus*, nursing.

Craig Tooley

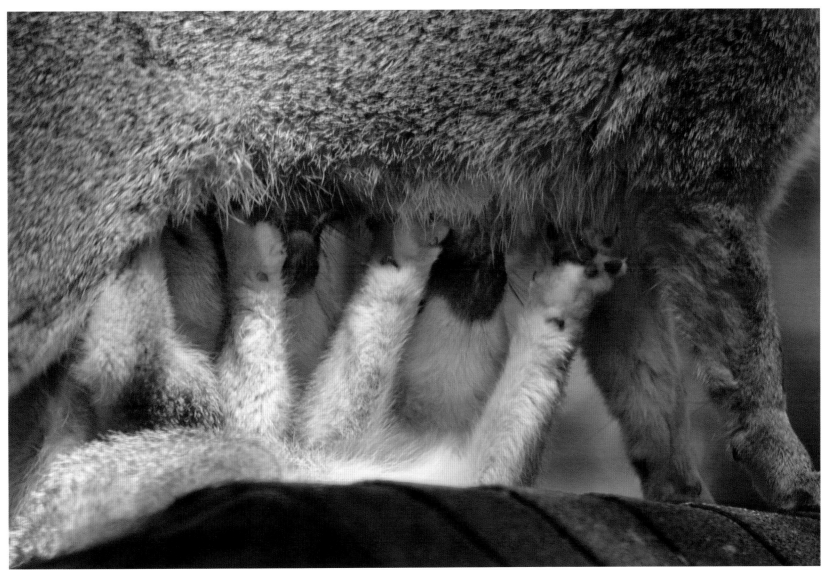

This little Gray Fox kit, *Urocyon cinereoargenteus*, is nursing in comfort on its back.

Craig Tooley

Buck, *Odocoileus hemionus columbianus*, in velvet in the early morning dew.　　Craig Tooley

Bucks begin appearing with their antlers in velvet. The velvet is a membrane that nourishes the growing antlers.

Fun Fact: If you could touch the velvet membrane, you'd find it hot to the touch.

Fawns continue to be born. Their exquisite beauty takes one's breath away. Often the mother will leave her newborn alone for a short time. Don't worry! She will return. Once in a while a Fawn is left alone in an unusual place.

Wildlife Encounter with a Newborn Fawn:

Newborn Fawn, *Odocoileus hemionus columbianus*, asleep on a road on The Sea Ranch.

David McFarland

" *I found this fawn on the road near our house. Mama was nowhere to be seen. I called The Sea Ranch Security and they placed cones around the fawn so that is would not get run over. Mama must have returned as it was gone about a half hour after Security left.* "

— David McFarland, The Sea Ranch

Wildlife Encounter with a Fawn:

" *It was a beautiful, sunny morning and I was on my morning walk near The Sea Ranch airport. Up ahead a Doe and two spotted Fawns crossed the road. As I approached, one of the Fawns walked back directly towards me, like a puppy dog. I felt its cold, wet nose on my bare leg and it proceeded to lick me with its soft tongue.*

" *I glanced at Mom, who was very agitated watching her baby. As I started to continue my walk, the Fawn seemed to want to join me, so I spoke to her gently. She went back across the road to join Mom and her sibling and we all moved on.*

" *Having always had a compulsive reverence for life, I felt honored.* "

— Janet Gerst, The Sea Ranch

When we interact with wildlife, the encounter touches us in ways we never imagined. May you be so honored!

The Coast is teeming with new life. There's a lush feel to the Coast right now. Take a deep breath and enjoy the fresh air.

Swallows are nesting now, including the striking Cliff Swallow.

Fun Fact: Cliff Swallows are aerial feeders. They eat flying insects.

Please try living with Swallows if they choose to nest near your home. They eat close to a thousand insects every day. If they nest in an inconvenient place, tack up a cardboard box under the nests to catch their waste.

Cliff Swallows, *Petrochelidon*, make gourd-shaped mud nests on cliffs, on buildings, and under bridges.

Craig Tooley

Cliff Swallow nests with cardboard boxes to collect the droppings.

Jeanne Jackson

94

This Barn Swallow, *Hirundo rustica*, seemed unperturbed by the comings and goings at Surf Supermarket.

Craig Tooley

One year a Barn Swallow pair built a beautiful mud nest on a light fixture just outside the entrance to Surf Supermarket in Gualala.

A Word to the Wise About Pruning and Tree Removal:

It would be wise to avoid pruning or cutting down trees at this time of year. One fellow had a large, dead Bishop Pine Tree cut down in June, not realizing there was an active bird's nest in it. The nest fell sixty feet to the ground. Miraculously the babies survived. They were four beautiful Brown Creepers that had to be driven to the Bird Rescue Center in Santa Rosa. If the tree removal had been delayed just a few weeks, these babies would have safely fledged.

Gualala Point Island, just off the north end of The Sea Ranch, is full of activity. You might spot nests of Western Gulls, Brandt's Cormorants and Pigeon Guillemots. More than a hundred Common Murres have been seen nesting on Bird Rock off Mendocino Headlands State Park.

Pigeon Guillemots are black and white seabirds. They spend their lives at sea except when they come ashore to breed on the rocks and islands off our Coast.

Fun Fact: Pigeon Guillemots have bright red/orange feet and dive for fish, using their wings to swim.

Another Fun Fact: It is not known where Pigeon Guillemots go for the winter. It is thought they go to the inland passage of northern British Columbia and southern Alaska but no one has ever documented that.

Pigeon Guillemots, *Cepphus columba*, are found along rocky coasts from Alaska to California.

Craig Tooley

Pelagic Cormorant, *Phalacrocorax pelagicus*, sitting on eggs soon to hatch.

Craig Tooley

Pelagic Cormorant nests tucked into cliff ledges are beginning to hatch chicks.

Wildlife Encounter with a Pelagic Cormorant Mother:

"*We watched an adult Pelagic wiggling and wiggling and looking unsettled. Finally a pointed beak and small head was visible under her tail. No wonder she looked unsettled!*"

—Diane Hichwa, The Sea Ranch

California Quail chicks arrive in June.

Fun Fact:
The California Quail is California's state bird. They mate for life and the male acts as a sentry, always watching out for danger.

Three California Quail chicks, *Callipepla californica*, with dad.

Craig Tooley

Steelhead have been seen this month, trapped in luxury, in the lagoon of the closed-to-the-ocean Gualala River. A walk along one of our wild rivers is the perfect antidote to whatever ails you, as our connection with Nature can bring great joy.

Wild pigs are found here too, though they are usually seen inland. These non-natives are designated game mammals in California. They are omnivorous.

Wild pigs, also called wild boar, *Sus scrofa*, eat almost anything.   Rozann Grunig

Wildlife Encounter with Wild Pigs:

" *I saw a herd of wild pigs on Skaggs Spring Road – at least 50, probably more. There were big ones, little ones, fat ones, tall ones, all rutting in the meadow. I drove by, rolled my window down and they could have cared less until they heard my voice. 'Hello, pigs!'*

" *They perked up their little ears and they high-tailed it out of there in all directions but my way. After the cloud of dust disappeared, there were two little pigs, as tiny as large cats, just looking as dumbfounded as me. It was a cute moment. Loved those pigs.* "

—Alisa Edwards, Anchor Bay

June is a good month to see Butterflies if the weather has been dry. Another large migration of Tortoise Shell Butterflies was seen near Annapolis. Several species of Swallowtails arrive and grace our gardens with their presence.

Western Tiger Swallowtail, *Papilio rutulus*,   Peter Baye
feeding on a Leopard Lily, *Lilium pardalinum*.

So we strive to appreciate each day, to notice the tiny wildflowers that could be so easily overlooked, to take time to watch the ocean, to inhale the fragrance of our redwood forests, knowing we are fortunate to be on the beautiful Mendonoma Coast as summer begins to unfold.

Spider web jewels.

Craig Tooley

Fun Fact: Spider webs are made of protein. Spiders will use the breeze to move the first strand across the space where the web is to be installed. Then they will carefully cross this first strand, spinning another strand on top of the first, as they begin to build their intricate webs.

Mendonoma Sightings Throughout The Year

People flock to the Coast for the Fourth of July festivities. Many also take time to enjoy what Mother Nature chooses to put on display every day. After the fireworks, barbecues and parades, you still have the Mendonoma Coast in all its glory, with the backdrop of the ever-changing, entrancing Pacific Ocean.

July often brings fog, especially in the mornings. The resultant moisture can reveal a work of art.

Encounter with Spider Web Jewels:

"*One silver-lining of this summer's foggy-drippies is the surfeit of bedecked and bejeweled fences and trees. One wee observer suggested this might be Cinderella's gown just after it was fashioned.*"

—Cathleen Crosby, Gualala

There are countless examples of Mother Nature's beauty just waiting for you to see with the eyes of a child.

The holiday weekend is a great time to kayak on one of the Coast's beautiful wild rivers. The Russian, Gualala, Garcia, Navarro, Little River, and Big River are treasures beyond compare. All these rivers, except the Garcia and Little River, are accessible and navigable by kayaks.

Being in Nature brings beauty and serenity into our lives, qualities that can't be bought, only cherished in our hearts and in our minds.

Rita Peck kayaking on the Gualala River.   Craig Tooley

A walk on a Mendonoma bluff can bring thrilling sightings.

Wildlife Encounter While Walking on the Gualala Bluff Trail on the Fourth of July Holiday:

" *I went to the Gualala Bluff Trail around 10:30 a.m. on the Fourth. The river was clear and you could see many Common Mergansers from the north end viewpoint near Trink's. It was as if the Mergansers were having their own 4th of July celebration. They scooted around, chasing each other, and then diving. The water was so clear you could see them swimming along the river bottom.*

"*Dave Hamilton came by with his dog. He reached into his pocket and presto – the harmonica was ready to go. He played the "Star-Spangled Banner" in honor of the occasion and mid-way through we had a flyover of three Brown Pelicans.*"

—Bob Rutemoeller, Gualala

Young Brown Pelicans are arriving from their breeding grounds, headed north. You can tell if they were born earlier this year by their brown heads, white under-parts and pristine wingtips. Adults have white heads and brown under-parts.

Fun Fact: Brown Pelicans in flight are relatively easy to photograph due to their large size and slow wingbeats. They use air currents off the waves for flying. In contrast to their seemingly effortless grace aloft, it takes these birds a great deal of effort to get up into the air.

A young Brown Pelican, *Pelecanus occidentalis*, with a brown head and white under-parts flies north with an adult.

Craig Tooley

There are handsome Gulls migrating along with the Brown Pelicans – Heermann's Gulls. These opportunistic Gulls are quite aggressive for their size.

Fun Fact: Heermann's Gulls nest on just a few islands in the Sea of Cortez off Mexico. They feed on small fish but they also steal fish from other birds. They have been seen going into the pouch of a Brown Pelican and stealing its catch. Now you know why they migrate with the Brown Pelicans!

A Heermann's Gull, *Larus heermanni*, lurks, waiting to steal a fish from the plunge-diving Brown Pelican, *Pelecanus occidentalis*.

Craig Tooley

You can't help but notice Bull Kelp that has reached the surface of the ocean. This form of brown algae grows from the bottom of the ocean floor in what is called holdfasts. The bulb at the unattached end has a portion of carbon monoxide in it, which helps it to float to the surface and obtain the sun it needs.

Many denizens of the sea use kelp forests for shelter and food. When kelp is ripped from its holdfasts and tossed up on the beach by winter storms, it provides food and shelter for sand crabs and such.

Fun Fact: Bull Kelp is quite nutritious and is used in sushi.

Bull Kelp, *Nereocystis luetkeana*, has reached the surface of the Pacific Ocean.   Craig Tooley

When the Pacific Ocean lives up to its name and is calm, wonderful sightings can be had.

Wildlife Encounter with Dolphins:

" *At first scan of the horizon this flat ocean morning, I saw what I thought was a new patch of kelp out a hundred yards or so from shore. The kelp beds begin to show up this time of year.*

" *But something about it was more alive than kelp and, whipping out my spotting scope, I could clearly see fifty or so large, dark dorsal fins meandering off The Sea Ranch, slowly moving south. They returned again, leisurely drifting among each other, sometimes breaking into playful leaps. They moved so that I could see their blunt heads and full sides which are lighter in color.*

" *They appeared to be Risso's Dolphins.* " —Ken Holmes, The Sea Ranch

Orcas have been seen in July off the south end of Gualala and off the Point Arena Pier. Summer also brings us occasional sightings of Humpbacks and the biggest creature of them all, the Blue Whale.

Wildlife Encounter with a Blue Whale:

Being in the right place at the right time is a wonderful thing. Linda Bostwick and Mel Smith achieved just that from the deck of their home. It was a half-hour before sunset when they spotted a Blue Whale straight out from the Point Arena harbor.

This huge whale burst head first out of the water, its gaping mouth open and its lower jaw bulging with seawater. To Linda and Mel's excitement, they were seeing this behemoth feed.

They watched it rise from the ocean again and again, never seeing the whale's tail, just its head and a portion of its body, which would sink straight back down into the ocean. Finally darkness pulled the curtain on their extraordinary floorshow.

Fun Fact: A Blue Whale calf consumes one hundred gallons of milk each day. It is rich in fat and the baby gains two hundred pounds a day.

Another Fun Fact: When the mouth of a Blue Whale is wide open a Bull Elephant can fit inside.

A Blue Whale, *Balaenoptera musculus*.

Craig Tooley

Abalone season is closed in July but divers are thinking about where they will dive next month. Don't bother asking where their secret spots are. Ab divers never dive and tell.

Fishing can be good this time of year. When the winds die down the Pacific Ocean can look like a lake. That's an invitation to fishermen and women to head out and see what can be found. A thirty-four pound Ling Cod has been caught north of Point Arena Cove. Big Salmon have been reeled in too as they have moved in closer.

Fun Fact: You can fish at the Point Arena pier without a license, though you do need to follow the California Fish and Wildlife regulations regarding size and limits. Perch is a common fish to catch there. You can also fish for Rock Cod, Herring, Sardines, Cabezon, Kelp Greenlings and the occasional Ling Cod.

Charles Zinser with a 27.5 pound Chinook Salmon, also called King Salmon, *Oncorhynchus tshawytscha*.

Jack Likins

A fishing boat and the setting sun.

Craig Tooley

The commercial fishing fleet might arrive and anchor off the Mendonoma Coast if the Salmon are running. At night their lights twinkle in the clear air. With all that goes on in our world, there is a comfort, a sense of rightness, in seeing the fleet ply our waters.

Birds are fledging and sometimes there can be problems with their beginning flying lessons. Common Raven young are particularly clumsy and quite raucous.

The Salal Public Access Trail on The Sea Ranch is a bird paradise. Fledgling Chestnut-backed Chickadees are being fed, along with Pacific Wrens fluffing their feathers to get their parents to deliver the goods. Salal Creek runs low in July but the cascades are usually still going. Wild Azaleas in whites, pinks and oranges make an appearance in sunny spots. It's a wonderland in there and the journey's end leads you to a path to a beach. Shouldn't all journeys end with a path to the beach?

A klutzy fledgling Common Raven, *Corvus corax*.　　　　Allen Vinson

Ospreys are beginning to fledge and their hungry cries fill the air. Common Murres can be seen streaming northward, flying low over the water and flapping hard and fast. They also are seen resting on offshore islands. Recently they have nested on rocky islands off the Mendonoma Coast.

There is a lot of activity going on with seabirds. You might see a courtship display, mating, nest building, eggs in nests, plus many downy chicks running up to their parents to be fed. A great place to observe these shy birds is at Gualala Point Island, which is just south of Gualala Point Regional Park. A Sea Ranch public access trail beginning at the park conveniently brings you to a bird's eye seat for watching the action from the bluff trail.

Fun Fact: Common Murres are affectionately called "Penguins of the North" due to their ability to walk upright. Their eggs are extremely pointed at one end, which helps keep them from rolling off a rocky ledge.

Common Murres, *Uria aalge*, fly low over the ocean, accompanied by two Brant's Cormorants.   Craig Tooley

Fun Fact: Black Oyster-catchers can be found on rocky outcrops and islands just off the Coast. They nest on the ground.

Important To Note:

The rocks and islands off the Mendonoma Coast are part of the California Coastal National Monument. No public access is allowed.

Black Oystercatcher family, *Haematopus bachmani*, an adult with three chicks.   Craig Tooley

Barn Swallows are among the many birds that are fledging this month.

Wildlife Encounter with Barn Swallow Fledglings:

" *We saw four Swallows sitting on the edge of our roof, looking like they were just hanging around. Then they all opened their mouths and a parent came to feed one of them. These were adolescents, out of the nest, but not ready to be gainfully employed. This may sound familiar to some of your readers!* " —Jonathan Raymond, The Sea Ranch

Barn Swallow fledglings, *Hirundo rustica*, waiting to be fed.   Craig Tooley

Once in a while a male bird will see its reflection in a window or a mirror. It sees a very handsome bird, a bird that could be competition. So it pecks at the reflective surface, trying to drive the bird away. Pulling a shade or covering the surface is usually all it takes to remove the "competition."

Wildlife Encounter with a Male Dark-Eyed Junco:

" *The mirrors on our vehicle were getting attacked by a little Junco daily. The little guy would fly up to a mirror in a most vicious manner. During his attack, a female Junco was perched above on a wire, chirruping him onwards – kinda like a sporting event.*

" *I enjoyed the event too, however our mirrors were taking a beating. How to stop the attack without hurting him was a challenge. I downloaded some pictures of an Owl from the web, cut them out the same size of our mirrors and placed the pictures on the mirrors.*

" *We then watched as the little Junco reappeared for the next attack. He darted down to the mirror, took one look at the frowning Owl, and quickly disappeared with his mate close behind.*"

—Eric Anderson, Anchor Bay

Dark-eyed Junco, Oregon race, *Junco hyemalis*, is primarily a seed eater.

Craig Tooley

Killdeer use dry gravel bars to lay their eggs. The stones and pebbles are good camouflage. This is one of many reasons NOT to drive in any river. How could you possibly spot these eggs from a truck or an ATV? Leave your vehicle behind and carefully walk the river. You will find that even deceptively barren-looking gravel bars are teeming with fish and wildlife that survive by hiding or using the gravel as camouflage.

Killdeer, *Charadrius vociferous*, eggs look like stones in the gravel.　　Richard Kuehn

Wildlife Encounter with a Killdeer:

" *I was walking on a gravel bar of the Gualala River near Twin Bridges when a Killdeer suddenly jumped up, made lots of noise and started walking away, dragging an apparent broken wing. Then it came back to within eight feet of me. I took a couple of steps closer and it fluffed up. Then it did the fake broken wing again and I saw that he was leading me away from four eggs.*

" *I later did some research and found that this is typical of Killdeers. They try to distract predators by flopping on the ground and dragging the wing and tail to show the white wing patches and orange rump. While doing this they make lots of noise while moving away from the eggs. If this doesn't work, they fluff up - I guess like us making ourselves 'big' when dealing with Mountain Lions.*

" *I went back a week later and the whole drama played out again.*"

—Rich Perry, The Sea Ranch

Fawns continue to be born. Triplets were seen on Stoneboro Road near Manchester. Care when driving is always a good mantra for the Coast.

Wildlife Encounter with a Doe and a Fawn:

Sue Hansen and Bobbie Penney were driving down Highway 1 when a Doe crossed in front of them. As Bobbie asked, *"Where is it? Where is it?"* Sue stayed at a stop, despite several impatient drivers behind her. Sure enough, a fawn then bounded across the highway.

Fawns, *Odocoileus hemionus columbianus,* follow their mothers across Highway 1.

Craig Tooley

One of the more unusual creatures we share the Coast with is the Rough-skinned Newt. You might catch a glimpse of its orange under-parts as it walks across a forest path. You never want to touch this Newt as it has a high level of toxin that can cause skin irritation.

Wildlife Encounter with Rough-Skinned Newts:

"*At the tiny stream paralleling Fort Ross Road to the north and turning north at the San Andreas Fault, I found a pool full of swimming Newts!*" —John Sperry, Timber Cove

Fun Fact: The only animal that can eat this Newt is a Garter Snake. They are locked in an evolutionary battle. The more the Garter Snake can tolerate eating the Rough-skinned Newt, the more this Newt evolves to protect itself with higher and higher level of toxins. In the Newt's case, it's truly overkill, as it has way more toxin than it needs to kill its prey.

Rough-skinned Newts, *Taricha granulosa*, live in fresh water and on the land.

Craig Tooley

116

And then there's the more benign Alligator Lizard.

Wildlife Encounter with an Alligator Lizard:

" *I have been splitting firewood recently, building a large stack for next winter. The woodpile has a new tenant already, even before the usual Chipmunks move in. She – he? – is a beautiful Alligator Lizard with shiny black and tan patterned skin that looks a lot like a miniature beaded purse.*

" *She now lives in the woodpile's buggy basement where my guidebook says she'll eat slugs, scorpions, centipedes, insects and spiders, including Black Widows. Bravo! I say. She should be safe and well-stocked in her new abode, when she's not out sunning on her porch.* " —Dorothy Ruef, Gualala/Ajo, AZ

Alligator Lizards, *Elgaria coerulea*, enjoy sunning themselves on warm rocks.   Craig Tooley

Once in a while a Sierran Treefrog will sneak under a door and pay someone a house call.

Wildlife Encounter with a Sierran Treefrog:

"*In my office is a framed photograph of a Costa Rican Tree Frog. I was dismayed one morning to find a real frog sitting on its picture. I couldn't figure out how he got in the house, much less across the room, up the wall and onto the frame.*

"*I took the frame outside and the frog climbed onto the picture and stared at it. Eventually I shook him off and left him in the garden. But the most amazing thing of all is three days later he was back in the room sitting on the frame in exactly the same place.*" —Peggy Mee, The Sea Ranch

Fun Fact:

We had a naming contest for this photo and the winner was Gail Hamilton with her caption – "Mom?"

A Sierran Treefrog, *Pseudacris regilla sierra*, on a framed picture of a Costa Rican Tree Frog.

Peggy Mee

Here and there, twined around a tree or bush, the first lovely blooms of our wild Honeysuckle, California Honeysuckle, can be seen, delighting our hearts with its delicate beauty.

Native grasses are tall and beautiful now. The bluffs at the Point Arena - Stornetta Public Lands or the meadows at Gualala Point Regional Park would be great places to see them undulating in the breezes.

Jeanne's Visit to the Point Arena - Stornetta Public Lands:

"*I wish I could wrap up the beauty of this part of the Coast and give it to you as a gift. The crashing surf, the wildflowers and the native grasses swaying in the breeze had us stopped with delight and wonder.*"

California Honeysuckle, *Lonicera hispidula*, has a very light fragrance.

Craig Tooley

A Mountain Lion, *Puma concolor*, sizing up its prey.   Craig Tooley

A Mountain Lion is occasionally seen in July. One has been seen in the Timber Cove area and another at The Sea Ranch.

Wildlife Encounter with a Mountain Lion Stalking a Gray Fox:

Jerry Erickson heard the resident Gray Fox pair making yipping sounds. One was standing up, looking towards a stand of trees. The other was calling from a neighboring property.

Jerry walked out to see what was going on and stood thirty feet away from a stand of Redwood Trees. There in the shadows he found a Mountain Lion in full crouch, with its head on its paws, staring steadily at the nearer fox.

"*I couldn't believe it. I did not want to turn my back so I slowly picked up some road gravel and let it go. I never saw an animal turn as quickly as that Mountain Lion did.*" As the Cougar left, of all things, the Foxes ran after it. Jerry has lived on The Sea Ranch for over forty years and has never seen anything like this.

Fun Fact: A Mountain Lion's back legs are slightly longer than its front legs. This allows the Cougar to jump horizontally or vertically.

120

If the weather warms up, Butterflies appear to grace us with their presence. What could be a more charming sight on a lovely summer day?

Fun Fact: These Butterflies are found from southern British Columbia to Mexico.

Mylitta Crescent Butterfly, *Phyciodes Mylitta*, dark male.

Craig Tooley

Our wildlife encounters enrich our lives in so many ways. To live with the wildlife that was here before us is our challenge and our privilege. And the more we learn about this special place, the more we appreciate its wonders.

An infrequent fogbow.

Craig Tooley

Mendonoma Sightings Throughout The Year

The sounds of summer on the Coast are crashing waves, Osprey calls, barking Sea Lions and the busy chatter of numerous American Goldfinches. Sometimes the sounds are muted with morning fog. When the fog pulls back the vibrant colors of the trees and the Pacific Ocean are revealed, as if for the first time.

Once in a great while the combination of fog and sun will bring a chance to see a fogbow.

Fun Fact: Fogbows are sometimes called white rainbows.

The beauty of the Mendonoma Coast has the ability to change a dark day into a bright one. Truly, you just have to pause to see what draws people from around the world.

Abalone season starts up again in August. Coupled with a morning low-tide, seekers of red treasure head for the ocean.

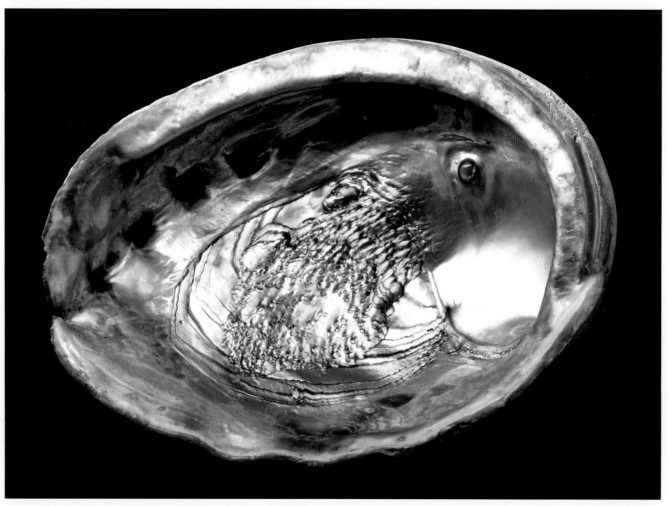

The iridescent interior shell of an Abalone, *Haliotis rufescens*.

Craig Tooley

Huckleberry bushes are ready for picking. As not all bushes have berries, look for bushes where American Robins, Hermit Thrushes and Swainson's Thrushes are feeding. They will show you where there are ripe berries. On the Mendonoma Coast, there are usually plenty of berries to share.

Fun Fact: Huckleberries are wild blueberries. They are often called Mother Nature's vitamin pills because of their high antioxidant levels.

Huckleberries, *Vaccinium ovatum*, ripen in August and continue ripening into autumn.

Craig Tooley

Dungeness Crabs thrive in the clean water off the Mendonoma Coast. Once in a while one will wander up on the beach. Don't be tempted to grab it and take it home for dinner. Their take is highly regulated.

Wildlife Encounter with Mating Dungeness Crabs:

Irene Leidner and her granddaughter, Maddy, were enjoying a leisurely walk on Bowling Ball Beach. It was high tide, which probably explains what they saw. Two Dungeness Crabs were on the edge of the surf, the larger crustacean on top of the smaller one.

As they watched and wondered what was going on, a dog came over and picked up the top crab by its claw. Irene said the dog proudly trotted down the beach with his treasure. Can you imagine what happened next? A loud 'yip' pierced the air. The crab had grabbed the dog on the lip with its other claw. The crab did let go and so did the dog. Irene retrieved the crab and put it back on the smaller one.

Irene's instincts were right. The crabs were mating. The larger one was a male. The smaller female had just molted and was ready to mate.

Fun Fact: A good size female Dungeness Crab can carry more than two million eggs. They mate from spring through fall.

A Dungeness Crab, *Metacarcinus magister*, seen on Walk-On-Beach, The Sea Ranch.

Craig Tooly

If there is a lot of krill in the ocean, Blue Whales will come this far north. It is said that if you see an island in the ocean where there wasn't one before, you've seen a Blue Whale. Because of their immense size, they do not come out of the water much at all. And you normally see only one or two at a time. Their spouts are enormous, leaving a lucky watcher no doubt about what she just saw. Summer on the Coast is the time to look for Blue Whales. They are among the most endangered of all cetaceans. While they are recovering from intense whaling of years past, their numbers are relatively small.

Humpbacks are also seen, but in greater numbers.

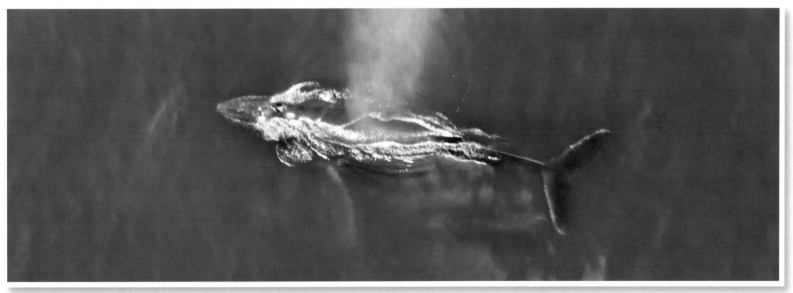

Humpbacks, *Megaptera novaeangliae*, visit the Mendonoma Coast more often in the summertime. Can you spot the baby, the calf, just below the mother?

Craig Tooley

Wildlife Encounter with Humpback Whales:

Natasha Lynn was seeing Humpbacks, lots of Humpbacks, from her home near Salt Point State Park. She drove to Fisk Mill Cove to get a better look. Her reward? She heard Humpback song, the hauntingly beautiful sound usually heard only underwater.

In 2010 a small group of young Gray Whales did not migrate. They spent the summer off the Mendonoma Coast. They are part of the new Pacific Coast Feeding Aggregation, a subspecies that doesn't migrate to the Arctic. The phenomenon continues to occur, giving locals and visitors alike a chance to see them up close and personal.

Jeanne's Wildlife Encounter with Young Gray Whales:

"*Three young Gray Whales were making appearances near Gualala Point Island and then cruising by the sandbar-closed Gualala River. Rick and I decided to see if we could spot them. With Huckleberry, our golden retriever, in the back seat, we drove to Gualala Point Regional Park. The breeze had swept away the fog. Whitecaps danced across the ocean and we thought it would be a miracle to see the Whales as their blows would be difficult to spot.*

"*We enjoyed the bluff walk nonetheless. Just as we were approaching the south corner of the park we heard something. Two humans and one fur-face stared out at the ocean. 'There!' I cried. 'I see it!' Rick answered. Closer in than we've ever seen them, two Gray Whales sliced through the blue water, showing us the length of their bodies, followed by a flick of a tail. What we had heard was the sound of their blow, an amazing, wonderful experience.*"

View from the bluff trail at Gualala Point Regional Park, looking south into The Sea Ranch with Gualala Point Island at the far right.   Jeanne Jackson

Two young California Gray Whales visited the waters right off the Point Arena pier.

A young Gray Whale, *Eschrichtius robustus*, swimming right next to the pier at Point Arena.

Deborah Heatherstone

Wildlife Encounter with a Gray Whale while on a Kayak Trip on the Russian River:

"*My wife, my sons and I paddled around Penny Island and headed out by the river mouth to see the Seals and the Pelicans. We pulled out on the sandy beach on the north side of the river mouth to have a sandwich. I wandered over the dunes and there, not ten yards offshore, was a whale.*

"*At first we thought it was in trouble but quickly realized it was just fine, rolling around in the shore break, perhaps rubbing its barnacles on the gravelly bottom. It was so close we could clearly see the blowhole. There were several spouts offshore in the sea stacks where the rest of the pod remained. It was a California Gray Whale, about thirty feet long. After about an hour it headed out to the others.*

"*I kick myself for not having my camera, although the images are firmly embedded in my memory.*"

— Timothy McKusick, Timber Cove

Dolphins and Porpoises can also be seen off the Coast. Pacific White-sided Dolphins have been seen near Gualala Point Island. Risso's Dolphins, with their rounded head, have also been spotted.

Wildlife Encounter with Surfing Dolphins at Gualala Point Regional Park:

"*I watched two Dolphins swimming and playing together in the surf at Gualala Point Beach. They were pretty close in, catching the curls of the waves, riding the waves, and then diving just underneath them. They were having the best time! The last time I saw Dolphins was over three years ago, so this was such a gift!*" —Christina Chapman, Gualala

We need our connection with Nature. It feeds our soul and brings us great happiness.

Risso's Dolphins, *Grampus griseus*, are sometimes called Gray Grumpus.

Ron LeValley

Fun Fact: Risso's Dolphins have no teeth in their upper jaws. They feed on fish, with the majority of their food being Squid. They can dive to a thousand feet and hold their breath for thirty minutes. However they usually make shorter dives of one-to-two minutes.

Another sight to behold in the ocean are Nudibranchs, sea slugs in fantastical colors.

Wildlife Encounter with Nudibranchs:

"Nudibranchs range in size from so tiny you can barely see them, to six-to-twelve inches or more. Around the Mendonoma Coast they are typically one-to-four inches long. There are many different kinds. They are usually colorful and fun to look for and identify. Look for their eggs and when you see the egg sacks or strings of eggs, then you know to slow down and start looking."

—Diver and underwater photographer Ken Bailey, Gualala

Fun Fact: There are over 3,000 species of Nudibranchs and they are found in all the world's oceans. More species are still being discovered. If you've seen one, you definitely haven't seen them all.

Opalescent Nudibranch, *Hermissenda crassicornis*, a colorful sea slug.   Ken Bailey

Brown Pelicans are still on the move in August, headed north. Many will travel all the way to the Gulf of Alaska. The decreasing amount of daylight in the months to come will trigger their return to Mexico. Young birds, born earlier in the year, are seen frequently now that they are strong enough to fly many miles.

Wildlife Encounter with Brown Pelicans:

"*Around 5 p.m. there were thousands of Brown Pelicans in and around the mouth of the Russian River. Approaching Jenner from the south, they were lined up along the utility wire spanning the river. Due either from the wind or from their constant exchanging places, the wire was swaying back and forth. In unison, the Pelicans were leaning forward, then backward, swinging on the wire in order to keep their balance. It was quite a sight!*"

—Richard Skidmore, The Sea Ranch

A juvenile Brown Pelican, *Pelecanus occidentalis*, rests on a bluff top.

Craig Tooley

Even as Brown Pelicans are still heading north, the start of the shorebird fall migration south has already begun. Amongst the species that can be seen are Black Turnstones and Wandering Tattlers. They fly thousands of miles in their twice a year migration, breeding in Alaska and Northwestern Canada and then migrating to the coasts of Baja California, Mexico and South America.

Fun Fact: This shorebird comes by its name – Turnstone – because it actually turns over stones and other objects to find food.

Black Turnstones, *Arenaria melanocephala*, are usually found in rocky habitat along our Coast. These are two non-breeding adults, identified by their lack of white facial markings, and are in the vanguard of the fall migration.

Craig Tooley

A fascinating animal that can be seen on the Mendonoma Coast is the Long-tailed Weasel. One has been seen in Irish Beach and another made a burrow next to one of the vacation cottages at the Point Arena Lighthouse. Their cute appearance might give you the wrong impression. They are fearless and aggressive hunters, seeking rodents, rabbits, small birds and occasionally fish.

Fun Fact: This weasel's eyes are black in the daytime but when caught in headlights at night, they glow emerald-green.

Long-tailed Weasel, *Mustela frenata*, peeks up from its burrow.

Dennis Latona

Paper Wasps build beautiful scalloped nests of chewed up wood fibers mixed with saliva. Once in a great while they will take over an empty birdhouse and make it their own.

Fun Fact: Once this has happened it is best to leave them be. In the winter the males will die off and the female can be more easily removed. Or perhaps a Skunk, which is a predator of these wasps, will take care of the situation by raiding the nest. To prevent Paper Wasps from building a nest inside a wooden birdhouse, tack a piece of aluminum foil on the ceiling.

Paper Wasps, *Polistes*, have papered over a wooden birdhouse for their nest.   Craig Tooley

River Otter mothers can be seen hunting and playing with their pups in August. Look for them where rivers, creeks and waterfalls meet the ocean.

Those pink flowers on tall thick stems blooming along Highway 1 in spots are Belladonna Lilies. The common name for these non-native flowers is Naked Ladies because the leaves bloom first and then die back. The flower then blooms on a naked stalk.

Fun Fact: Along with being beautiful, they are delightfully fragrant.

Naked Ladies, *Amaryllis belladonna*, thrive in sunny spots along Highway 1. Craig Tooley

A number of wildflowers are pointing the way to autumn. Poison oak growing in full sun is turning shades of red. Solomon Seal berries are turning purple-blue. Andrew's Clintonias are sporting cobalt-blue berries.

Andrew's Clintonia, *Clintonia andrewsiana*, berries are a vibrant blue.   Craig Tooley

Black Oystercatcher young are fledging, as are Common Murres. Gualala Point Island is a perfect place to observe them.

Common Murres, *Uria aalge*, with a Western Gull, *Larus occidentalis*.

Craig Tooley

Fun Fact: When Common Murre chicks hear their fathers' calls, they are led towards the water, and they instinctively hurl themselves off of the cliffs. It is a true leap of faith as they don't yet know how to fly. They will swim away from their nesting island with their fathers and learn to fly in a couple of weeks.

Near Point Arena, a Mountain Lion leapt across Highway One. And a young one visited The Sea Ranch.

Wildlife Adventure with a Young Mountain Lion and a Brave Housecat:

"*It was an incredible sighting. I have glass French doors opening to the front yard and, as I came into the room, I could see a large, buff-colored feline sunning himself on a PG&E box! His tail was quite long and thick, but you could tell he was a juvenile Mountain Lion because of his enormous tail, size, the dark markings on his cheeks, and some fading spots on his coat.*

"*We opened the door to get a better look and watched the animal walk for a bit. The Cougar seemed to be distracted, watching us and what turned out to be a neighbor's housecat, Truffles. Truffles, also called 'Saddam' because she takes on anything and everything, entered the picture and started to stalk the young Mountain Lion.*

"*She ultimately tried to attack the Mountain Lion and they moved off into the brush and out of sight, but you could hear the yowls of fighting cats. Truffles survived, albeit a little shaken, and I haven't seen the beautiful Mountain Lion since.*"

—Lynne Barnard, The Sea Ranch

Mountain Lion, *Puma concolor.*   Craig Tooley

139

MENDONOMA SIGHTINGS THROUGHOUT THE YEAR

We are fortunate to be in a place that has very little light pollution. Sky watchers of all ages are in for a treat mid-August. Usually around the 12th and 13th is when the Perseids meteor shower peaks. And if it coincides with a new moon, the show could be amazing.

On clear nights it is possible to see the International Space Station fly across the face of the moon. You can find out where it is at heavens-above.com. This website shows many space events, including comets. You can also learn the latitude and longitude of any town on earth. Gualala's latitude is 38.766 and longitude is 123.427.

The night sky also gives talented photographers an opportunity to capture the nocturnal beauty of the Mendonoma Coast.   David "Sus" Susalla

Ospreys can be seen fishing in the Pacific Ocean or in rivers for fish to take back to their mates and their offspring who are still in their nests.

Osprey, *Pandion haliaetus*, heads back to the nest to feed his offspring.   Craig Tooley

Our experiences with nature enhance our lives in myriad ways. And the beauty of summer on the Coast will work its way into your heart and mind, never to release you from the spell.

Autumn

This is the time of year when the oak leaves dance in the breezes and the ocean swells begin to crash against the shore. Even the sunlight is different, imparting a golden glow to our surroundings. You can see, hear and feel the beginning of autumn.

A Wandering Tattler, *Tringa incana*, looking for tasty insects.

Craig Tooley

Mendonoma Sightings Throughout The Year

September is a wonderful time to be on the Coast. Seeing a whale spout, watching the sunset, or laughing out loud at the dance of a Wandering Tattler can lift your spirits and bring you joy – priceless gifts from the Mendonoma Coast.

Fun Fact: These birds teeter and bob while searching for food on the shoreline. They earned the name "tattler" because they sound an alarm when a predator is near. They arrive from points north and overwinter on the Coast.

This is also the time of year that makes the hearts of birders beat a little faster. Yes, the fall migration is in full force. Some of the shorebirds that you might see now are Turnstones, both the more common Black and the less common Ruddy, and Red-necked Phalaropes, spinning around in the water like windup toys as they feed.

Fun Fact: Red-necked Phalaropes breed to the north of Alaska along the shores of the Arctic Ocean and will migrate all the way down to South America for the winter. They occasionally make an appearance in such places as the ponds at The Sea Ranch Golf Course or near the Point Arena Pier.

Red-necked Phalaropes, *Phalaropus lobatus*, spin to stir up food.

Craig Tooley

Some of the other migrating water birds to look for are Western Sandpipers, Sanderlings, Sooty Shearwaters, Geese, Willets, and Whimbrels.

Fun Fact: It is rare to see Shearwaters from land. However they do feed near dolphins, whales, and other groups of seabirds. So train your binoculars when you see any of these creatures feeding and you might also find Shearwaters soaring just over the waves nearby.

Fun Fact: If you live where Milkweed – the host plant for the Monarch Butterfly – is native, planting some would be like putting out the welcome mat. If you live on the Mendonoma Coast, planting native nectaring plants, especially Manzanita, would be very beneficial.

Monarch Butterfly, *Danaus plexippus*, the very essence of beauty, feeding on a Butterfly Bush, *Buddleja davidii*.

Jeanne Jackson

The magnificent Monarch Butterflies are also migrating. Monarchs only live four-to-five weeks with one exception. Every year in September or October they produce a Methuselah generation that lives seven-to-eight months. This is the generation that has begun its very long migration to points south.

If the weather is warm with no wind, and the sardines or anchovies are running, there might be a sighting of Bottlenose Dolphins.

It is rare to see a Blue Whale. However, a mother Blue Whale and her calf have been spotted off Point Arena. Humpback Whales, on the other hand, are often seen off the Mendonoma Coast in September.

The tail and back of a Humpback Whale, *Megaptera novaeangliae*.   Craig Tooley

Wildlife Encounter with Humpback Whales:

"*Two Humpbacks seemed to be frolicking. They breached fifteen to twenty times, as if trying to outdo each other. It was as if one whale said, 'You think you can do this?' before it breached quite spectacularly.*"

—Ted and Soili Ochsner, Timber Cove

Gray Whales are also seen, especially the new group of young Gray Whales that didn't migrate north but stayed just off the Mendonoma Coast. Instead of turning over mud for amphipods, as they do in the Arctic Circle, this new group suctions these shrimp-like crustaceans off rocks. This is an exciting development for those of us whose hearts thrill at seeing them.

Wildlife Encounter with a Young Gray Whale:

"*Over Labor Day weekend two of our grandchildren were body surfing at Anchor Bay Beach when they spotted a juvenile Gray Whale. I don't know if it was their excited shouting that brought the curious whale closer.*

"*The kids never dreamed that they would be boogie boarding with a whale, a once in a lifetime experience.*"

—Gail Thompson, Gualala

Wildlife Encounter with a Gray Whale and Her Calf:

Two Gray Whales, *Eschrichtius robustus*, spouting.   Craig Tooley

"*I watched them from the Gualala Bluff Trail behind Surf Supermarket. The mother whale did an up and flop – a complete breach. I wanted to shout but there was no one around but me.*"   —Dan Laux, Gualala

Take some time and wisely spend it in nature. You may have an experience that will last a lifetime. And it's okay to shout.

An unusual mushroom usually fruits in September. It's the Dyer's Polypore.

Fun Fact: This mushroom helps to break down dead wood. It is also used by dyers of yarn. When young, as in this photo, it dyes yarn yellow or orange. As the mushroom ages it turns brown and gives dye-makers rich browns for their yarn.

Dyer's Polypore, *Phaeolus schweinitzii*, is usually found growing on Bishop Pine or Douglas-fir.   Craig Tooley

We often get a heat wave this time of year though it never lasts long. With the warmth thousands of tiny bugs will hatch and spiral into the air, as if dancing to music only they can hear.

Wild Blackberries are ripe and ready to stain your hands and lips while pleasing your senses. Huckleberries continue to ripen. The sight of bushes loaded with these wild blueberries can transport you into giddy Huckleberry heaven. Many birds and four-legged creatures feast at this table too.

Two young Raccoons, *Procyon lotor*, eyeing a laden Huckleberry bush.   Craig Tooley

Kate and Jack Matull with Rockfish, *Sebastes*.   Siegfried Matull

Abalone diving can be very rewarding this month. If the kelp is thick, that is a good sign for the growth and weight of Abalones. The availability of abundant food means the Abalones will be at their biggest.

Fishing can also be great in September.

Wildlife Sightings:

"*It has just been the most beautiful time of year – foggy mornings breaking into warm crystal-clear afternoons, the occasional slow-rolling Humpback Whale cruising by, the nightly Osprey giving fish their last tour of the sky, kelp beds growing thicker and wider, and lots of fishermen out there enjoying long, lazy days.*"

—Grace Steurer, Point Arena

An unusual sighting can occur on a summer evening with a very dark, moonless sky and no nearby lights. You might see the sparkling lights of bioluminescence on the Pacific Ocean.

A wave lit with bioluminescence.   Ron LeValley

Fun Fact: Bioluminescence in the ocean is caused by tiny, single-cell bioluminescent organisms, most often dinoflagellates. This shows that tiny organisms, together in vast numbers, can create an astonishingly beautiful phenomenon.

An Experience with Bioluminescence:

"*Laverne and I went out onto our deck around 10 p.m. to look at the clear sky and the ocean, and we were treated to a phenomenon that we had never seen here before. The ocean was alive with light all the way out to the horizon, making every whitecap look like a twinkling star in the water.*

"*The waves that hit Robinson Reef were like ribbons of bright white light on the top of the ocean. It looked like there was no ocean anymore, just an endless galaxy of stars that went all the way to the edge of the coast below us.*

"*We stood there awestruck with the Milky Way overhead. It was a truly magical night!*"

— Mark Hancock, Gualala

Turpentine weed is flowering in the drier gravel bars of the Gualala River.

> **Fun Fact:** Don't smell it! The aroma is as strong as smelling salts and smells like turpentine and vinegar mixed together. As if to compensate, Mother Nature gave it beautiful spikes of lavender flowers.

Fringed Corn Lilies are also in bloom.

Turpentine weed, *Trichostema laxum.*   Peter Baye

Karen Tracy and Nan Brichetto find a Fringed Corn Lily, *Veratrum fimbriatum*, in bloom amidst ferns.   Jeanne Jackson

> **Fun Fact:** Fringed Corn Lilies are plants found only in Sonoma and Mendocino Counties. This Lily was growing near Gualala Point Regional Campground. The trail to Cook's Beach is another place to see these beauties. The huge leaves, so handsome in the spring, are now shredded and riddled with holes. Native plants, like this endemic Lily, feed native insects.

We continue to learn about how all things are interconnected. Mother Nature has important lessons if we but listen.

Another late blooming wildflower is the rare King's Gentian.

If you wonder what ships and boats are passing by the Coast, you can find their names and their speed at marinetraffic.com. Passenger vessels show up in blue. And as cruise ships are repositioning this month – ending their Alaska cruises and heading for Mexican waters – you will be able to see quite a few of these "birthday cakes lit with thousands of lights" on their way.

King's Gentian, *Gentiana sceptrum*, is found on wetland meadows.

Craig Tooley

Encounter with A Fata Morgana:
Sometimes you look out over the ocean and you can't believe your eyes. Rich and Nancy Trissel saw a mirage from their home in Gualala. Rich described it thusly: "*It looked like a city, or sometimes a large Arizona mesa, hovering above or just touching the ridgeline of the ocean.*"

Fun Fact:
Fata Morganas are real optical phenomena and can be photographed. Mirages happen when light rays are bent, producing an image in the sky.

Fata Morgana mirage over the ocean fog.

Rich Trissel

Another phenomenon that can be photographed by a lucky photographer is the green flash. September can be prime time to see one at sunset.

The green flash can't be bought or owned, but it can be stored in your memories to be cherished anytime you need a sparkle of beauty in your life.

The green flash at sunset.   Craig Tooley

The Ospreys leave near the end of September. We are comforted in knowing that they will return, trumpeting the arrival of spring. And we can hold in our hearts that we are fortunate to live or visit where Ospreys choose to nest.

Ana Sanchez surfing off Moat Creek.

Craig Tooley

Mendonoma Sightings Throughout The Year

Leaves fall along forest paths, softening footfalls and filling the air with a fresh scent. The ocean is speaking too, as storms to our north make their presence known with crashing waves. Autumn on the Coast can touch you in ways that will last a lifetime.

When the big waves hit, ocean mist floats across Highway 1 as the bluffs tremble with the Pacific Ocean's force. Then intrepid surfers head for the waves off Arena Cove and other surfing spots, grins fixed on their faces.

High waves begin to wash over the sandbar and into the Gualala River lagoon.

Fun Fact: This is a very advantageous condition for Steelhead. Juveniles have a chance to adjust to salinity gradients in the lagoon in preparation for their journey into the ocean, once the river opens again.

Saltwater enters the Gualala River lagoon.

Jeanne Jackson

Steelhead Trout, *Oncorhynchus mykiss*, in the Gualala River.

Craig Tooley

Indian summer arrives this month and visitors and locals alike rejoice in the warm golden days followed by crisp evenings. We are lulled for a while. We know there are changes to come but for now the living is easy.

Fun Fact: Some Native peoples called this heat wave in the fall "Person's Summer."

Autumn sunsets are to be savored. Many drivers along Highway 1 will pull over to watch Mother Nature's floorshow.

Moments like these are a specialty of the Mendonoma Coast.

October sunsets can last for what seems like forever.

Jeanne Jackson

October is prime time for the rut, the mating season of the Columbian Black-tailed Mule Deer. The males are sporting their racks, their antlers.

Each year they lose their antlers and need to regrow them in the spring and summer. Velvet is a membrane that nourishes the new antlers. In the autumn the velvet has been rubbed off and the hard bone remains.

Give these big Bucks a wide berth. They only have one thing on their minds.

Wildlife Encounter with Bucks:

"*Two Bucks are chasing all the gals around my field. The poor Does are running for dear...or shall we say deer...life.*"

—Adrian Bennett, The Sea Ranch

Fun Fact: The western count for a Buck's rack is used here. Only the tines of one antler are counted. With the eastern count the tines of both antlers would be counted.

A healthy, four-point Buck, *Odocoileus hemionus columbianus*, on a coastal bluff. Peggy Mee

Varied Thrushes, Yellow-rumped Warblers and Golden-crowned Sparrows are migrating to the Coast in larger numbers.

Fun Fact: In the summer months, Varied Thrushes eat insects. When they arrive on the Coast they switch to berries and seeds. They will often eat the last of the Huckleberries.

Another Fun Fact: Male birds some-times sing in the fall, mistaking the good weather for mating season.

Varied Thrushes, *Ixoreus naevius*, are sometimes mistaken for American Robins.

Craig Tooley

Abalone diving can be good in October though the abundant kelp makes it difficult to navigate underwater.

The inside of an Abalone shell can be spectacularly beautiful.

Fun Fact : Though very uncommon, an Abalone will occasionally produce a beautiful pearl. The biggest one ever found was discovered by a diver off the coast of Mendocino. It measured 5.51 x 3.14 x 1.57 inches.

The inside of this Abalone shell shows iridescent mother-of-pearl.

Craig Tooley

This horn-shaped pearl of the Red Abalone, *Haliotis rufescens,* is quite valuable.

Craig Tooley

There are three types of Abalone pearls - shell pearls, blister pearls, and gut pearls. A gut pearl is started within the Abalone when a piece of sand or other tiny object is forced inside. These rare pearls are prized for their beauty and make striking jewelry.

Sometimes an Abalone pearl is hiding in plain sight. If you know what to look for on the beach you might find a prize of your own.

Fun Fact: Abalone pearls are called opals of the sea.

An Abalone pearl washed up on the beach.   Craig Tooley   Here is the same Abalone pearl after it was peeled   Craig Tooley
                                                                           by a jeweler to reveal its beauty.

You might see a splash of vibrant orange hanging from a tree or bush. Wild Honeysuckle vines are sporting clusters of gorgeous orange-red berries.

Fun Fact: These berries are not edible for humans. They are very bitter; birds and deer rarely eat them. Consequently they stay on the vine to delight our senses.

The pink flowers of Pink Honeysuckle, *Lonicera hispidula*, have turned into orange-red berries.

Craig Tooley

Wild Turkeys can be seen in grasslands along Highway 1. They are game animals in California and, with a license, can be hunted at certain times of the year.

Wildlife Encounter with Wild Turkeys:

Jon and Susan Sandoval have a large group of Wild Turkeys, males and females, near their home in Gualala. The males have somehow got it in their minds that Jon's car, a Mini Cooper, is a threat, possibly a rogue male Turkey.

When Jon drives down his road, the tom Turkeys chase it from behind, apparently believing they are protecting the females. Jon makes it safely to the garage and puts the garage door down. The Turkeys then look at each other as if to ask, *"What are we doing here?"*

Jon is tempted to drive the Mini Cooper to where the females are clustered. He calls to Susan, *"Let's go get their women!"*

Wild Turkey, *Meleagris gallopavo*, squawking.　　　　　　　　　　Craig Tooley

Turkey Vultures get their name because their heads resemble a Turkey's red head. They are year round residents on the Coast. They are Mother Nature's garbage collectors, as they eat carrion. It can be startling to come across one or more with their wings extended.

Fun Fact: They perch with their wings extended to warm themselves but the sun is providing double duty – the heat burns away bacteria.

Turkey Vultures, *Cathartes aura*, are sometimes called Buzzards.   Craig Tooley

Another Fun Fact: On the ground a group of Turkey Vultures is called a venue. If flying they are called a kettle.

Another startling sighting might be Harvestmen, also called Daddy Longlegs, bunched up in a snarl – a quiet snarl. They are seen more often in the autumn, hence their common name refers to them being seen around harvest time.

Fun Fact: Harvestmen are in the family Arachnida but they aren't spiders. They only have two eyes as compared to spiders that have six or eight. They are harmless to humans.

Harvestmen, *Opiliones*, tangled together for protection and/or warmth.

Craig Tooley

Praying Mantises, *Mantodea*, eat many insects and are an important part of our ecosystem.

Craig Tooley

Another unusual creature on the Mendonoma Coast is the Praying Mantis, from the group called Mantids.

Wildlife Encounter with a Praying Mantis:

"*Depending on the species and size they eat everything from mice to aphids. They get their name from their posture of 'praying' with their forelegs. But if you are one of their prey, don't be fooled by this devout name. They'll snatch you from the air sooner than look at you!*"

—Ken Holmes, Sacramento

Fun Fact: Praying Mantises can change color, from green to brown, to help camouflage themselves in their surroundings.

Not So Fun Fact If You are a Male Praying Mantis: When mating or immediately afterwards, female Mantises eat the head of the male. It is believed this helps nourish the newly formed life in the female.

The peak of the Orionid meteor shower is around the 20th of October. To find the exact peak, go to www.space.com.

Jeanne's Encounter with a Orionid Meteor Shower:

"*I sat in the dark watching the brilliant flashes of light streak across the sky. The Sea Lions on Fish Rocks kept me company with their barking, while the crashing waves of the ocean added an occasional punctuation mark. A feeling of gratitude filled me and I gave thanks to be on our special Mendonoma Coast.*"

Fun Fact: The Orionid meteor shower is from the debris left behind by Halley's Comet.

A meteor streaks across the night sky.

Ron LeValley

173

The first storms can arrive in the latter part of October and they often bring rainbows – big arching ones and short prism-like ones. Mother Nature paints in the sky, using many of the colors on her palette. If we have enough early rains, the possibility of edible mushrooms such as *Boletus edulis* has mushroom foragers checking their favorite spots.

Large flocks of Greater White-fronted Geese can be seen migrating south. Aleutian Cackling Geese will follow, along with California Gulls and Surf Scoters, among others.

Wildlife Observation:

"*I am not sure if it always holds true, but I always sense that the fall storm door opens soon after the arrival of these migrating White-fronted Geese.*"

—Bob Keiffer, Hopland

Fun Fact: Greater White-fronted Geese fly in a wandering V over land near the bluffs. They honk as they fly. Eventually they will take a left turn and head east to overwinter in the Sacramento Wildlife Refuge or elsewhere in the Central Valley.

Greater White-fronted Geese, *Anser albifrons*, eat seeds, grain, grasses, sedges and berries.

Richard Kuehn

Monarchs, the king of all Butterflies, continue to migrate to points south, many to the mountains of central Mexico. They are miracles of nature, in that they are the only known Butterfly species to fly a round-trip migration of nearly three thousand miles.

Fun Fact: Journey North tracks the Monarchs' migration, as well as Gray Whales, American Robins, Hummingbirds and other birds and mammals. You can participate in this citizen science by posting your sightings at www.learner.org/north.

Monarch Butterfly, *Danaus plexippus*, looks for nectar.

Craig Tooley

The world of nature that surrounds us tells many stories. It's our pleasure to listen to these stories and to continue to learn of all the great connectivity that binds us together.

October on the Mendonoma Coast can bring precious memories strung together like a string of pearls, a lovely necklace of memories of one of the most beautiful places on Earth.

One of the many seasonal creeks on the Mendonoma Coast.

Craig Tooley

November

Mendonoma Sightings Throughout The Year

What a joy it is to walk along a creek listening to the various sounds the water makes as it tumbles, slides or crashes on its journey to the Pacific Ocean. It is Mother Nature's way of creating a symphony. All you have to do is listen to her music.

The first significant rains usually occur in November. The ponds of our seasonal creeks slowly begin to fill. When they are full, they will spill over and bring the creeks to life.

If enough rain falls, the Gualala River will open to the Pacific Ocean for the first time in months. Young Steelhead will be released from the river to begin the next stage of their lives, and adult Steelhead will return to the newly opened river to spawn.

Fun Fact: When the Gualala River is closed to the ocean for the summer and early autumn, the mouth of the river is called a lagoon. When the river is open to the ocean in the late autumn and winter it is called an estuary. When the river opens for the first time, it only takes an hour to drain the lagoon.

Gualala River breaching the sandbar for the first time in months.

Jeanne Jackson

With enough rain, the king of all edible mushrooms makes a dramatic appearance gladdening the hearts of coastal mushroom foragers. *Boletus edulis*, commonly called King Bolete, can be found in Bishop Pine forests. It is also known as Porcini or Cep and is one of the most satisfying mushrooms to find and one of the most delicious to eat. One Mendonoma mushroom aficionado described it thusly, "*The first taste is everlasting!*"

Mushroom Adventure:

"*I went hunting with Patty McBratney and found Boletes in a grove of Pine Trees. I cut open the older ones to ensure there were no bugs. I found one that I didn't pick. It was old and probably not good for eating, but the top of it was the size of a dinner plate. I was surprised to find one so large this early, but I'm learning not to let Mother Nature surprise me anymore – she can do whatever she wants!*"

—Rozann Grunig, The Sea Ranch

Fun Fact: Many creatures feast on wild mushrooms, especially King Boletes. It's best not to pick all you find, leaving some for our wildlife.

King Bolete, *Boletus edulis*, has a sponge-like layer of tubes underneath its cap instead of gills.

Cathleen Crosby

Shaggy Manes, *Coprinus comatus*, are edible and delicious. Craig Tooley

Later in the month, with enough moisture, Chanterelles and White Chanterelles, Coccoras and Matsutakes might also be found fruiting.

Shaggy Manes have also appeared this month, often right alongside roads.

Fun Fact: Shaggy Manes quickly deliquesce into an inky black puddle. They are edible when young, as in the photo here.

Gray Whales can be seen on their journey south to Baja California. Look for the telltale white puff from their blowhole and then watch for a glimpse of their back, followed by their tail.

The tail of a Gray Whale, *Eschrichtius robustus*, with its distinctive notch in the middle.　　　Ron LeValley

Several huge Blue Whales, with their extremely tall spouts, have been seen cruising by Gualala Point this month.

Fun Fact: Blue Whales are the largest animals on the planet. They can be as long as two school buses. Blue Whales are usually seen singly or in pairs. They are perhaps the largest animals ever to have lived on the planet, including the largest dinosaurs.

Blue Whale, *Balaenoptera musculus*, as seen from an airplane.

Craig Tooley

Risso's Dolphins and Pacific White-sided Dolphins have been seen in November. If the ocean is calm, look for a line of darkness in the water. You might find a huge school of fish with hundreds of birds diving and feasting. Just in front of the fish you might also find dolphins or porpoises. The dark line itself might be a pod of dolphins. It can be rewarding to pay attention to anomalies on the ocean.

Locals and visitors alike never take dolphin, porpoise, or whale sightings for granted and we want to share the excitement. It's part of enjoying the gift of this time on the beautiful Mendonoma Coast.

Fun Fact: Dolphins sleep with only one-half of their brain at a time and sleeping dolphins can be seen with one eye closed. After a while, they will open the other eye and close the open one. They alternate this way throughout their entire nap.

Pacific White-sided Dolphins, *Lagenorhynchus obliquidens*, can often be seen in large pods, sometimes over one thousand strong.

Ron LeValley

Sunset watching is a Coast tradition and there are many places to pull over along Highway 1. If you are driving through Gualala as the sun begins to set, pull over and head to the Gualala Bluff Trail. You can walk in through the parking lot of the Surf Motel or to the left of Breakers Inn.

No video game or television show can compete with the beauty of a Mendonoma sunset, the yellows and oranges will eventually be replaced by shimmering reds. It can last fifteen minutes or more.

When you watch the sunset, you have the opportunity to see the elusive green flash.

Green Flash Sighting:

"*I saw one that flashed like a green LED.*"

—Steve McLaughlin, Gualala

Sunset near Cook's Beach, north of Gualala.   Craig Tooley

The lack of light pollution on the Mendonoma Coast is something to celebrate. It makes for wonderful stargazing.

Mid-November brings the Leonid meteor showers and the show can be breathtaking. The best way to watch is simply to lay back and allow your eyes to adjust. As you wait for the "shooting stars," allow yourself to fall under the spell, to feel grateful, and to be at peace. These are incomparable gifts of the Mendonoma Coast.

We share the Coast with many creatures. North American River Otters live near the mouths of our rivers and streams. They swim in the ocean and rivers, plus they can maneuver on land.

River Otter, *Lontra canadensis*, in the kelp and waves.

Craig Tooley

Wildlife Encounter with River Otters:

"*Rita and I spotted three River Otters off of Shell Beach. The discovery of these delightful River Otters frolicking and feeding off our wonderful coastland brings much joy. They seem to play and play with such abandonment that it gives us delight that lasts the entire day and night.*" —Craig Tooley, The Sea Ranch

If conditions allow, November ushers in the Dungeness Crab season. You might see the lights of the fishing boats at night as hardworking fishing crews endeavor to bring this delicacy to market.

Fun Fact: Colorful floats on the ocean surface are sure signs that Dungeness Crab season has started.

Crab traps ready to be deployed and a working Crab boat at sea.

Craig Tooley

Sea Urchins thrive in the clean waters off the Mendonoma Coast.

Encounter with a Sea Urchin Diver:

Alan Lawson is a commercial fisherman who goes out of Point Arena with a partner. Sea Urchin diving is dangerous, exhausting and tests a person's fitness.

Lawson dives in 10 to 60 feet of water, occasionally going as deep at 90 feet. He harvests underwater for an hour or two, and then resurfaces to rest on the boat for a half-hour. On a typical day he will spend four to six hours underwater and harvest over 2,000 pounds.

About half of these Sea Urchins go directly to Japan and the rest go to sushi restaurants in the United States. As you watch the ocean today, have a thought for our ironmen of the deep.

Purple Sea Urchin, *Strongylocentrotus purpuratus*. Sea Urchins are an important fishery along the West Coast.

Craig Tooley

Fun Fact: Sea Urchins are covered in purple or red spines. Underneath the spines is a beautiful white shell. Inside the shell is the roe, the edible part. It is called uni in sushi-talk.

Great-horned Owls, *Bubo virginianus*, hunt at night.

Craig Tooley

We share the Coast with several species of Owls, including Northern Pygmy-Owls, Western Screech-Owls, and Great-horned Owls.

Fun Fact: Great-horned Owls are the only animals that regularly eat Skunks.

Another Fun Fact: Great-horned Owls do not build their own nests. They take over an existing bird's nest in a tree or use a snag or hollow.

November is the last month of the year's Abalone season, though the ocean can be too rough for all but the most experienced divers. Before a storm, however, the ocean can be calm, giving Abalone divers an invitation they can't refuse.

Abalone isn't the only prize. Lingcod will make a fisherman's day too.

Richard Lewis with Lingcod, *Ophiodon elongates*, and a 10.5 inch Abalone, *Haliotis rufescens*.

Jack Likins

We share the Coast with the ever fascinating Common Raven. One of the most intelligent birds, you will be constantly amazed by their antics.

Wildlife Encounter with a Raven and a House Cat:

"*I swear this is true. Delores and I were inside our home looking out toward the ocean through the redwoods that line the front of our small deck. Our cat, Mick, was sitting on the deck rail, enjoying the sights, as were we. All of a sudden a young, medium-sized Raven landed on a limb directly in front of Mick. They were separated by approximately two feet. The Raven looked at Mick and…started chanting.*

"*I swear it sounded just like the sound in the 1977 film 'Close Encounters of the Third Kind.' The Raven's squawk was not loud but very soothing and muted. Kind of like 'da, da, da, da, da…'*

"*Mick began replying with a very mellow 'meow, meow, meow.' This went on for about five minutes. They actually looked like they knew each other. Delores and I just sat in awe watching this unique situation between our Manx cat and the coal-black Raven.*"

—Eric Anderson, Anchor Bay

Fun Fact: You can tell a Common Raven from an American Crow by its much larger bill, longer length and greater wingspan, and its diamond-shaped tail. American Crows are rarely seen on the Mendonoma Coast.

Common Ravens, *Corvus corax*, have many different vocalizations.

Craig Tooley

Common Ravens are particularly brazen, even keeping company with a much bigger California Sea Lion.

Fun Fact: Common Ravens are acrobatic fliers. They will perform rolls and summersaults in midair. They can actually fly upside down. Young Ravens play with sticks, dropping them and diving down to catch them before they reach the ground.

Common Raven, *Corvus corax*, peers over the back of a California Sea Lion, *Zalophus californianus*.

Craig Tooley

A Black Bear might ramble through the area this month, perhaps eating the last of the huckleberries or apples on an old Gravenstein Tree.

Also feasting on the last of the berries are Black Phoebes and Varied Thrushes, which are migrating through our area. Gulls, Surf Scoters and Common Loons are migrating south, as are Brown Pelicans.

So graceful in the air, Brown Pelicans can be rather clumsy when coming in for a splash landing. You can watch them landing in the Gualala River in the late afternoon. You will be hard pressed not to laugh out loud.

Brown Pelican, *Pelecanus occidentalis*, coming in for a landing.   Craig Tooley

Raccoons are known for their intelligence though some consider them pests. They are very photogenic and their antics can make you smile.

Wildlife Encounter with an Impudent Raccoon:

"*My husband, Ken, and I noticed a young Raccoon in a tree beside our deck. As I went to take a photo of it, the sassy Raccoon stuck its tongue out at me!*"

—Ann Davis, The Sea Ranch

You might see a swarm of thousands of insects after a rain this month. These insects look like small ants with large wings. When they land the wings fall off.

Wildlife Encounter with Flying Insects:

"*The bugs you are seeing are termites. Their reproductive members – queens, males – have recently developed from nymphs and since they are such weak flyers they only come out when the humidity is just right, before or after rainfall, and the winds are calm. After their flight and mating, their wings are no longer needed and fall off.*"

—Entomologist Marion Sandoval, Berkeley

A young Raccoon, *Procyon lotor.*   Craig Tooley

Bobcats are seen on gopher patrol in meadows along the Coast. Once in a while one will take a rest in the waning afternoon sunshine.

Wildlife Encounter – A Great Day:

"*There are good days and then there are great days. Mana and I were in Manchester, delighted to fill our baskets with Boletes and stumble upon a beautiful 4-point deer antler. In all my life hiking in nature I have never found one.*

"*Then, while heading back to our car, a large gorgeous Bobcat ran across our path just a few yards away.*

It was my first sighting of such a wild cat – truly a fine specimen!

"*Then, just to top off our day of wonder, we coasted into our driveway to find a huge Buck standing in front of our house. Mother Nature sure was puttin' on a show!*"

—Sabina Walla, Anchor Bay

Bobcats, *Lynx rufus*, are about twice as big as the average housecat, though their size varies.

Craig Tooley

Storms in November will begin the process of ripping Kelp from its underwater holds on rocks.

Encounter with Kelp:

" *We live at 1,200 feet, two miles as the crow files from Stillwater Cove. We've seen dark, elongated thingamabobs that we cannot identify. They are perhaps 15-35 feet long and thin, parallel to shore, but at some distance. Might they be lines of Kelp?* "

— Richard Gross, Stillwater Cove

Bull Kelp, *Laminariales*, is an annual plant – it completes its life cycle in one year.

Craig Tooley

Richard was definitely seeing Kelp. Some are still attached waiting for their date with Mother Nature. The Kelp, which is known as Bull Kelp, then gets washed up on our beaches. It's called Bull Kelp because it looks like a bullwhip when dried out in the sand.

Fun Fact: Underwater Kelp forests give shelter to more than 800 kinds of marine animals, including California's state saltwater fish, the bright-orange Sunfish, or, more properly, the Garibaldi. The Golden Trout is the freshwater state fish. A fun web site, which bills itself as an educational web site for kids of all ages, is oceansforyouth.com.

Garibaldi, *Hypsypops rubicundus*, is California's state saltwater fish.

Ken Bailey

In aboveground forests, here and there, an old growth Coast Redwood Tree has survived the logging of the late 1800's. These ancient trees are more precious than the finest jewels, standing sentinels to centuries long past.

Fun Fact: The McCabe Tree grows alongside the Gualala River. In the canopy of old-growth Redwood Trees is a world unto itself. A fascinating book to learn more about the world's tallest trees is *The Wild Trees* by Richard Preston.

The McCabe Tree, perhaps the oldest old-growth Redwood Tree, *Sequoia sempervirens*, on the Mendonoma Coast.

Chris Poehlmann

The close of November marks the end of the rut for our Black-tailed Deer and the big Bucks will be moving away.

Buck, *Odocoileus hemionus columbianus*, in a meadow.   Craig Tooley

The big swells from storms bring smiles to surfers, as there are several prime surfing spots on the Mendonoma Coast. Booming surf creates a mist that can reach across Highway 1 and drift up various canyons, an amazing sight indeed.

Big waves hitting the Coast.   Craig Tooley

Once a storm has abated, you can venture out and see what changes Mother Nature might have made to her furniture on Mendonoma beaches.

Abundant splendor perfectly describes autumn on the Coast. We have much to be thankful for as all things great and small are occurring here in November on the beautiful Mendonoma Coast.

Winter

Crisp, cold mornings with the early sky painted in soft pastels, frost on shaded rooftops, and the sweet scent of wood smoke in the air. The unmistakable call of a Pileated Woodpecker trumps all other bird calls as the Mendonoma Coast awakens to winter.

Pileated Woodpecker, *Dryocopus pileatus*, looking for its favorite food – ants.

Craig Tooley

December

Mendonoma Sightings Throughout The Year

One of the most exotic birds we share the Coast with is the Pileated Woodpecker. This prehistoric-looking bird is our area's largest Woodpecker and it has a big territory, around two hundred acres.

It's been said the call of a Pileated was the basis for the laugh of Woody the Woodpecker. It isn't an exact match, that's for sure, but once you've learned the call of the Pileated you will never forget it.

FUN FACT: The holes dug by Pileated Woodpeckers are rectangles. These birds are year round residents of the Coast. Leaving a dead tree, a snag, on your property may draw this striking bird into view.

One of the secrets of the Mendonoma Coast in December is the beautiful weather between storms.

You can experience a sun-drenched day and, if the horizon is clear, a green flash at sunset.

Sunny weather between storms.   Craig Tooley

December is a perfect month to stargaze. The stars shine brightly on the Mendonoma Coast. In mid-December look for the Geminid meteor showers. The lack of light pollution makes the Coast the perfect place to watch them. Anytime the night sky is clear is a good time to stargaze – it's a Coast tradition!

For those who know edible mushrooms, there is a veritable feast in the forest this month. Early in December King and Queen Boletes, *Boletus edulis* and *Boletus aereus*, can be found by lucky foragers.

Boletus edulis is one of the most desirable wild mushrooms. To find them, go on a mushroom hunt a week or two after the first several inches of rain. Look for a group of Bishop Pine Trees down a swale. Sometimes these large mushrooms can be found growing under Manzanita or Huckleberry bushes, but there will be Pines nearby. Salt Point State Park is a place where it is legal to forage. The current limit within this state park is five pounds of wild mushrooms per day.

Fun Fact: Drying King Boletes and then reconstituting them in water or wine intensifies their flavor.

Another Fun Fact: This mushroom has a Banana Slug feeding on the bottom of it and has several bites taken from the cap. Wild mushrooms feed many insects and animals of the forest.

King Bolete, *Boletus edulis.*

Craig Tooley

205

Jeanne's Perfect Day In The Forest:

"*Rick and I, accompanied by our golden retriever, Huckleberry, had a perfect day. The sky was brilliant blue and the ocean was calm. There had been enough rain and we were on a mushroom hunt. We looked for Bishop Pine Trees – Boletes need Pine rootlets to grow on. We ambled down a draw and it wasn't long before we were rewarded.*

"*I spotted a large one and turned back to Rick, exclaiming, 'Be still my heart!' It's that exciting to find one. It's like finding a jewel in the forest. As the hunt went on, we found eight of them, seven were in pristine condition, but the remaining one had mostly gone to bugs.*

"*On the way back home, Huckleberry had a dip in Quinliven Creek. That* pretty much makes a Golden Retriever's day. As I sliced the mushrooms in preparation for drying them, setting aside a portion for that night's dinner, I felt gratitude – gratitude for what Mother Nature provided, and gratitude for this most perfect day that I was able to share with Rick and a certain golden.*"

An abundant harvest of King Boletes, *Boletus edulis.*   Jacquelynn Baas

Many other edible mushrooms fruit this month, including Matsutakes and both white and yellow Chanterelles, Hedgehogs and Black Trumpets. Coccoras are pushing through redwood duff. Their striking yellow caps with a gauzy, white top are quite beautiful.

Not So Fun Fact: The poisonous Destroying Angel resembles the Coccora, but lacks its creamy top. Mistaking one for the other can have dire consequences. The Coccora should only be eaten by the most experienced forager, one who learns all of this mushroom's characteristics. Otherwise, it would be better to just enjoy its beauty as you pass by in the forest.

Oyster mushrooms and Pig's Ears are making an appearance. A strikingly beautiful mushroom, the Fly Amanita, catches one's eye with its bright red coloring and white spots. It's beautiful to look at but not to eat – at least without proper preparation, which involves boiling several times to remove the water soluble toxins.

Fun Fact: This mushroom appears on Christmas cards and New Year's cards as a symbol of good luck. They also were featured as dancing mushrooms in the Disney classic *Fantasia*.

Coccora, *Amanita calyptroderma*, is found in forests with Madrone nearby.

Jeanne Jackson

Fly Amanita, *Amanita muscaria*.

Craig Tooley

207

December can bring wild storms and crashing surf. The waves are so beautiful yet so dangerous. Standing a respectful distance from the bluff edge and taking in the majesty of the Pacific Ocean is an incredible experience. Its pure power and beauty can chase away what troubles you and lift your spirits, a gift that is yours to receive.

After a storm you might want to take a walk and see what Mother Nature has tossed up on one of our beaches.

Storms bring big waves.   Craig Tooley

An enjoyable excursion would be to see the sea tunnel and wave action at Hearn Gulch, which is at mile marker 10.08. You can park at mile marker 10.00, which is just north of Iversen Road in Mendocino County, and is the entrance to the Hearn Gulch coastal access. To see the sea tunnel in action you need to go at mean tide as there is little action at low or high tide.

Encounter with the Wave Action at Hearn Gulch:

"*The day we were there, a storm was coming in and the waves were BIG. Each time a wave hit the blow hole, there was a super loud "BOOM" that made the sand below us shake. We were so fascinated we stood there for what seemed like hours until it was getting dark and we really had to leave. I knew we were in a force of nature and grateful to experience it.*"

— Rozann Grunig, The Sea Ranch

Crashing waves at Hearn Gulch.

Rozann Grunig

You might also want see if Al, the Laysan Albatross, has returned to the waters off Arena Cove in Point Arena. This world famous bird usually returns by early December. Birders from all over the United States and even other parts of the world have come to Point Arena to add this bird to their life list.

Wildlife Encounter with Al, the Laysan Albatross:

"*I went up to see if I could see the Laysan Albatross that has been occasionally reported at the Point Arena Pier for several years. I arrived about 1:30 pm. On my way out to the pier there was quite a nice painting on plywood of my target nailed to the pier railing complete with the English and Latin names. I asked one of the fishermen if he knew about an albatross that hung out here. He said, 'Oh yeah, Al's here. I saw him over there just a few minutes ago.'*

"*This would be a lifer so my heart raced a bit as my hands raised my binoculars in search of the wayward bird. Not seeing him, my feet moved me to the end of the pier and I scanned the water.*

"*About a hundred yards out, floating near a channel marker ball, Al sat on the water sleeping. He was about the same size as the ball. Huge. Black and white. Bobbing. Shortly, he pulled his pink bill out and shook his head, then flew to about 100 feet from the end of the pier.*

"*Clear day, looks were great. Near tears.*"

—Ed DeBellevue, San Rafael

Al, the Laysan Albatross, *Phoebastria immutabilis* – a special visitor to our Coast.   Craig Tooley

Commercial Dungeness Crab season usually flourishes this month and fresh Crab will be available, if conditions allow, at Noyo Harbor, the Point Arena Pier and sometimes near the Gualala Hotel. The pristine waters off the Coast make for delicious Crab. On the other hand, Abalone season closes this month and won't reopen until April.

Fishing boat loaded with Crab pots heads out.   Craig Tooley

This month hundreds and hundreds of Steelhead and Salmon have been seen heading up the Garcia River.

Black Bears don't hibernate here on the Coast so a sighting of one isn't unheard of but it is infrequent. However a couple on the north end of The Sea Ranch woke up to find a Black Bear looking at them through the window as they lay in bed. Talk about an eye opener!

A Wildlife Encounter with a Black Bear:

Ted and Freda Noble heard a noise outside their Gualala home late one night. Expecting to see a Raccoon or a Skunk, they were surprised to see a large Black Bear hanging from the side of their house. It was trying to knock down their birdfeeders.

"*Banging and shouting did not disturb him at all. He just looked at us and went on hitting at the feeder until he managed to knock it down. The next morning we found our hummingbird feeder and birdfeeder on the ground. Empty!*"

—Freda Noble, Gualala

Black bear, *Ursus americanus*.   Craig Tooley

December is a good month to see Peregrine Falcons as they overwinter here on the Coast. One particular place to see them is around Gualala Point Island. A Peregrine Falcon was seen this month buzzing a group of Grebes on the Gualala River.

Wildlife Encounters with Hawks:

"*My husband, René, passed away a little over five years ago and he loved Hawks and Eagles. He said every time I see one around me it would be his spirit watching over me and I believe this is true.*" —Rose Tavitian, Manchester

Peregrine Falcon, *Falco peregrinus*, on Gualala Point Island.   Craig Tooley

Two Red-tailed Hawks, *Buteo jamaicensis*, soaring over the Coast.   Craig Tooley

It is uncommon to see a Golden Eagle, though one has been spotted this month in Point Arena. Varied Thrushes continue to migrate through the area. Great Egrets and Snowy Egrets are full-time residents of the coast.

Fun Fact: The key to telling Egrets apart is this: Great Egrets have yellow bills, Snowy Egrets have black ones.

Another Fun Fact: The Great Egret is the symbol of the National Audubon Society. Audubon was formed, in part, to stop the killing of birds for their feathers. The plumes of the Great Egret were so favored that 95% of these birds were taken. Laws now protect them and their numbers have vastly increased.

Great Egret, *Ardea alba*, wading into the Gualala River, looking for a fish.   Craig Tooley

California Gull, *Larus californicus*, at play.   Craig Tooley

One of the Coast's most common Gulls in the fall, winter and spring is the California Gull.

Fun Fact: This is the Gull that saved Mormon settlers in Utah from a plague of grasshoppers. In Salt Lake City a golden statue of this bird was erected in memory of this event. The California Gull was also honored by becoming the state bird of Utah.

Wildlife Encounter with Surfing Gulls:

"*Two of us watched a gang of a half-dozen Gulls in storm seas. These birds hung out together waiting for some monster wave to come along. When it did, they – in complete disorder – flew to it. Once the wave was well formed and the updraft along its front had teased a full curtain of spray, those guys were winging along parallel to the front, ahead of the updraft curtain.*

"*When the wave finally broke, every one of them would cut into the updraft and go zooming up fifty feet or so! I almost heard, 'Whoa! Cool!' The gang played that game, and I'm virtually certain it was a game, over and over again.*"

—John Sperry, Timber Cove

Tundra Swans may be arriving near the mouth of the Garcia River if we have had enough rain.

Tundra Swans, *Cygnus columbianus*, overwinter on the Garcia River floodplain.

Craig Tooley

When the ocean is calm enough, Gray Whales can be seen headed south. This is the very beginning of the southward migration and you are more likely to see this in the latter part of December. Dolphins have also been seen, sometimes in the hundreds, also swimming south. Any day is a good day when you are fortunate enough to see Dolphins or Whales.

Orcas have also been seen in December.

Wildlife Encounter with Orcas:

Mark and Laverne Hancock spotted a pod of Orcas between Robinson Reef and a line of crab buoys.

"*There were five to six adults, and they were extremely active – spyhopping, tail flashes and full leaps out of the ocean. They frolicked for about 15 to 20 minutes then they suddenly calmed down, moving very slowing northward.*

"*We noticed a dolphin-sized dorsal and realized there was a baby in with the pod! Given how small the baby was when we finally did start seeing it, we speculated that perhaps the initial commotion of the pod was because the baby was being born.*

"*It was one of the most breathtaking and awe inspiring times we have ever experienced. From the time we started watching them to when they finally went out of sight was an absolutely magical 1 hour and 45 minutes.*"

—Mark Hancock, Gualala

Orcas, *Orcinus orca*, also called Killer Whales, have very large dorsal fins.

Ron LeValley

Mountain Lions are rarely seen, as they are shy and elusive. However, they can occasionally be observed during the day hunting deer, their favorite prey. And they are sometimes seen at night on the Mendonoma Coast, usually illuminated by a car's headlights.

Wildlife Encounter with a Mountain Lion:

Denise Otterman and Bob Wrubel saw something flash ahead of their car as they were driving to their home on The Sea Ranch late at night. Denise called out, *"Slow!"* thinking it was a Deer.

As they slowly drove up, they saw it was a Mountain Lion. Denise described it as, *"beautiful and sinewy, long tail, long body and muscular."* As they approached, the big cat jumped the fence. She said it was *"like liquid gold, flowing over the fence effortlessly. Then it turned and looked at us."*

As if that wasn't enough then a *"huge Owl lit by our headlights flew over. The hunters were out that night! It was scary and exciting, an out of time, out of place, out of body experience."*

Bobcats are seen more frequently than Mountain Lions.

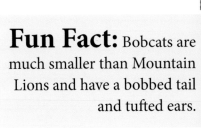

Fun Fact: Bobcats are much smaller than Mountain Lions and have a bobbed tail and tufted ears.

Bobcats, *Lynx rufus*, are seen in meadows hunting rodents. This one is about to cross a trail on The Sea Ranch.

Craig Tooley

Great Blue Herons are one of the most photographed birds on the Coast. They are about four feet tall and their wingspans can reach a width of six feet.

Fun Fact: In the air Great Blue Herons have very slow wingbeats and they tuck their neck in, creating an "S" shape. With their legs dangling behind, they are unmistakable in flight.

Great Blue Heron, *Ardea Herodias*, takes flight.

Craig Tooley

River Otters are seen year round. They eat fish, shellfish, small mammals and birds.

Wildlife Encounter with Harbor Seals and a River Otter:

"*I was exploring the beaches of Sea Ranch with my friend Jamie when we came upon a cove where we saw a group of eight Harbor Seals very close to shore all looking at the beach.*

"*As we entered the cove we interrupted a River Otter who had come to shore and was struggling with a large fish. We watched him for a while, as did the Seals, as he went up on some rocks, back into the water and then back to the rocks trying to eat this very large lunch.*

"*It was a magical stormy day! Unfortunately, I am writing this from Berkeley, but I always feel like I leave my heart on the Mendonoma Coast.*"

—Paul Burns, Berkeley

River Otter, *Lontra canadensis,* eating Octopus.   Craig Tooley

The Mendonoma Coast is blessed with clean air. One way to tell is by observing all the beautiful Lichen growing in the trees. Lichens are very sensitive to air pollution so it's a good sign to see them in abundance. Some people believe they harm trees but this is not so. Lichens are not parasites like Mistletoe, they are actually beneficial. Because people see dead or dying trees covered in lush Lichen they assume the Lichen is to blame. In fact, the Lichen can grow so abundantly on dead trees because it is able to get more light.

Fun Fact: Some Lichens are two or even three species – a fungus, an alga and a bacterium. Lichen is an amazing form of life.

Lichens growing on a tree limb.

Craig Tooley

There is a group of rocks off of Anchor Bay called Fish Rocks with an active and very vocal California Sea Lion community. They are full-time residents of the Coast. Every once in a while a Sea Lion will haul out on a beach or a bluff.

Wildlife Encounter with a Sea Lion on the Beach:

"My husband and I are frequent vacationers and wanna-be residents of Gualala. On a recent trip, we saw lots of wildlife including Harbor Seals, many Deer, and a handsome California Sea Lion on Shell Beach in The Sea Ranch.

"After spending about a half hour at one end of the beach, we decided to walk down to the other end of the beach and almost stumbled upon a Sea Lion resting way up the beach against the rock. He let out a loud grunt/snort as we approached, and the four of us – two dogs, two people – must have jumped back about two feet in surprise!

"We quickly left him alone. He seemed to be basking in the sun and I worried that he might be ill, but he was gone the next day."

—Jackie Gai, DVM, Vacaville

If you ever come across an injured Sea Lion or Harbor Seal, the proper thing to do is call the Marine Mammal Center at (415) 289-SEAL [(415) 289-7325]. Never take matters in your own hands!

California Sea Lion, *Zalophus californianus*, basking in the sun.   Craig Tooley

Another creature that is a full-time resident of the Coast is the Gray Fox.

Fun Fact: Gray Foxes are also called Tree Foxes for their great ability to climb as they have semi-retractable claws. They can even climb a telephone pole.

Gray Fox, *Urocyon cinereoargenteus*, on a stump.   Craig Tooley

Fetid Adder's Tongue, *Scoliopus bigelovii*, is in the Lily family and has distinctive mottled leaves.

Craig Tooley

Winter has just begun but the first of our earliest wildflowers, the Fetid Adder's Tongue, also called Slink Pod, has begun blooming on the forest floor. These tiny, brown, three-petal flowers are easy to miss but a joy to find.

Fun Fact: Once the leaves are mature, you will notice them as they are up to 12 inches long and mottled. But the exquisite flower is long gone, leaving a seed pod which is found hanging down on the ground, giving this California native its other common name, Slink Pod.

And the earliest of the Manzanitas are just beginning to bloom. With their exquisite upside-down urn-like white flowers, Manzanita blossoms provide food for insects and hummingbirds that fly year round. The waxy leaves protect the blossoms from rain and the flowers allow access for Anna's Hummingbirds, Butterflies, Bees and other insects.

Things You See Along Highway 1 in December:

"*Orange flames of burn fires glowing against the green and gray landscape, silver Foxes running through the grass, mushroomers searching for treasure in the woods, and an iridescent halo around the moon shining through the black lace of Redwood Trees at night.*"

—Wendy Bailey, Gualala

For many of us, the holidays are a time of gathering together. One of the best presents might not be found under a Christmas tree.

You might find it in the grace of a Brown Pelican riding a thermal, the subtle symphony of a creek, the amazing big voice of the tiny Sierran Treefrog or the sight of an enormous, barnacle-encrusted Gray Whale arching through the water. All these gifts, and so very much more, are yours here on the Mendonoma Coast.

Manzanita, *Arctostaphylos*, blossoms provide sustenance in the winter.

Craig Tooley

Tundra Swans, *Cygnus columbianus*, overwinter on the Mendocino Coast.

Craig Tooley

January

Mendonoma Sightings Throughout The Year

Our encounters with nature bring a touch of magic into our lives. If you are here on the Mendonoma Coast all it takes is a walk on the wild side to catch some magic of your own.

January finds the beautiful Tundra Swans in residence at the Garcia River floodplains if we receive enough rain. Their yearly return from the far north of Alaska and Canada is a welcome sight and an affirmation of the continuity of life.

Given enough rain our creeks and rivers make their presence known in the Pacific Ocean where you can see fingers of muddy water extending into the sea. Sometimes, at high tide, the Garcia River will flood at Highway 1, making the drive north a challenge.

FUN FACT: These snowy white Tundra Swans mate for life. Their breeding grounds are several thousand miles north in the Arctic.

Great Egrets, Peregrine Falcons, thousands of Gulls, and White-tailed Kites are here. You can also look for Red-shouldered Hawks, Cooper's Hawks, Varied Thrushes, and Western Bluebirds. Dark-eyed Juncos arrive en masse to overwinter. A few Brown Pelicans have yet to migrate for the winter. Look for the beautiful Harlequin Ducks near Gualala Point Island. A Golden Eagle and a Bald Eagle have been seen in January.

Ferruginous Hawks overwinter on the Mendonoma Coast.

Ferruginous Hawk, *Buteo regalis*, soaring.

Craig Tooley

Fun Fact: Ferruginous Hawks are America's largest Hawks. They hunt for mammals, such as rabbits.

Female Anna's Hummingbird, *Calypte anna*.

The male Anna's Hummingbird is already beginning to display for his ladylove, flying straight up into the sky and then plummeting down. Just before the little bird might plow into the ground, it pulls up, hovers, and makes a chirping sound with his tail feathers beside a tree where the female is watching.

Cooper's Hawk, *Accipiter cooperii*.

Fun Fact: Cooper's Hawks are excellent fliers, zipping through trees to capture an unsuspecting bird. One of these hawks might show up at a bird-feeder looking for an easy meal.

Fun Fact:

All three of these birds are year round residents of the Mendonoma Coast.

Fun Fact: White-tailed Kites hover over meadows, looking for their favorite meal - small mammals.

White-tailed Kite, *Elanus leucurus*.

All photos by Craig Tooley

229

Al, the Laysan Albatross, can be seen between storms off the Point Arena Pier. No one knows where this unique visitor goes during the storms. Perhaps to a safe, yet secret, cove or out to sea. Laysan Albatrosses are able to handle rough seas.

Handsome Al, the Laysan Albatross, *Phoebastria immutabilis.*   Craig Tooley

A Wildlife Encounter with Jellyfish, Whales, and Al:

"*Friend Fred McElroy and I paddled out of Point Arena Cove. It was beautiful water. We went out three or more miles to get in the whale lanes, paddled north maybe two miles, just short of the Lighthouse. We saw wonderful stuff!*

"*Water was magnificently clear – huge, pale, translucent Jellyfish, like live flowers, fields of them, vanished into the depths. We saw weird, dark, diffuse, outrageously tall blows yet another three or so miles out in the edge of a fog bank. The blows had to have been exaggerated, mirage-like, at least five-fold! We think they were south-heading Grays.*

"*But the real prize was our early visit with Point Arena's visiting Laysan Albatross, Al. He swam right up to us and gabbled something neither of us understood. He's one handsome dude, I tell you.*"

—John Sperry, Timber Cove

Fun Fact: Jellyfish are among the oldest living creatures on Earth, thriving for over 650 million years. They depend on currents, tides or wind for horizontal movement. They can move vertically by taking water into their bell shape and then pushing it out.

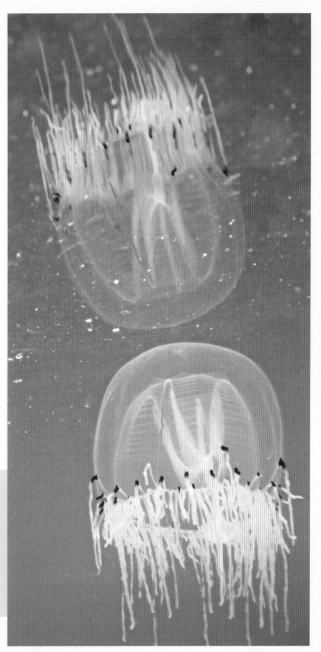

Bell Jellies, *Polyorchis*, seen just off The Sea Ranch.

Craig Tooley

When you are on the Coast it's wonderful to watch a storm approach. You might notice the first few clouds appearing from the north. The horizon often becomes sharp, like a knife edge, the low clouds chased away by winds. The surface waters of the ocean are driven by the southerly winds to move northward. But don't be fooled - the California Current always runs north to south. So if the ocean looks like it has changed direction, it can portend a storm.

Storm clouds, waterfalls, and a turbulent Pacific Ocean.

Craig Tooley

Storms also bring huge waves. It's a thrill to be safely standing on a bluff and experience the sight, feel and sound of the ocean crashing on the beach and the cliffs. At this time of year there is nothing 'pacific' about this ocean.

Big waves hitting Gualala Point Island.

Craig Tooley

Between storms, the horizon is often clear, giving you a chance to see the green flash at sunset. Watch for the moment the sun sinks below the horizon. If the conditions are perfect you may see an emerald glow enveloping the top of the departing sun. It doesn't flash across the horizon. It's as if someone on the other end of the sunset held a flashlight glowing green. Don't blink. It's over in a flash!

It's possible to see several green flashes during a sunset.

Double green flash.

Craig Tooley

If the Gualala and Garcia Rivers "green up," there's a possibility for catch and release fishing of Steelhead. Eleven pound Steelhead have been caught and released on the Gualala River this month.

The Gualala River turns "Steelhead Green." Hundreds of Gulls dot the sandbar [top of photo] and splash in the river.

Jeanne Jackson

January is prime time to see Gray Whales migrating south. Over 19,000 Gray Whales will pass by the Coast on their way to Baja California. They are usually further out on the trip south and stay down longer as they don't have calves with them. These magnificent cetaceans swim fifty-five straight days to reach their destination. Look for a spout and then train your binoculars on that spot to see a glimpse of its back, followed by its tail. If you are very lucky you might see a breach, where the whale jumps so that much or all of its body comes out of the water.

Jeanne's Wildlife Encounter with a Breaching Whale:

"I was at one end of our house, looking out a small window which overlooks the ocean. Suddenly a whale breached. Excited, I called out to my husband, Rick, but he didn't hear me. Imagine the power of the whale propelling itself out of the ocean, water sluicing off its body, followed by the booming sound as its enormous body then hits the water. Your pounding heart will confirm that you saw something truly spectacular."

Fun Fact: Some of the best places to spot Whales are at the bluffs at Navarro Point Preserve, the bluffs at the Point Arena Lighthouse, the outlook at the north end of Fisk Mill Cove at Salt Point State Park, or in a window seat at The Sea Ranch Lodge.

Visitors to the Gualala Bluff Trail have seen several breaches, along with spyhopping. Spyhopping is when the whale raises its head straight out of the water and appears to take a good look around. Another theory is the whale is listening for the surf break so it can check its position.

Spyhopping Gray Whale, *Eschrichtius robustus*.   Ron LeValley

A Wildlife Encounter with Gray Whales:

David and C'Anna Bergman-Hill were on the Gualala Bluff Trail when they spotted several Gray Whales just off the beach near the Seacliff Center. David photographed one of the Whales while the jogger kept his head down and missed a great sighting.

Oblivious jogger and a Gray Whale, *Eschrichtius robustus*.   David Bergman-Hill

Dolphins can also be seen heading south. Look for an anomaly on the ocean, perhaps a circle, a dark line or roiling water. Often that will be Dolphins.

Fun Fact: Risso's Dolphins follow the huge Humboldt Squid. As they prey on these Squid, they often get scratched from Squid beaks. Adult males turn almost white with age.

Risso's Dolphins, *Grampus griseus*, swimming fast and headed south.   Craig Tooley

Harbor Seals and California Sea Lions are in residence, along with the occasional Elephant Seal. On a calm day the barking sounds of the colony of male Sea Lions on Fish Rocks off of Anchor Bay can be heard at least a mile inland.

California Sea Lions, *Zalophus californianus*, on Fish Rocks.

Craig Tooley

Fun Fact: Do you know how to tell a Sea Lion from a Harbor Seal? Sea Lions are black when wet, brown when dry, have ears, and make a barking sound. Harbor Seals are gray when wet, white with black splotches when dry, and have no ears, just an opening, and they do not bark.

Killer Whales, Orcas, with their tall dorsal fin and black and white bodies, have also been seen this month.

Jeanne's Wildlife Encounter with Orcas and Sea Lions:

"*While watching Orcas through my spotting scope, I saw a large group of Sea Lions swimming frantically towards a beach just north of Fish Rocks. Behind them were two Orcas, looking for a mid-day meal.*"

This is also prime time for Dungeness Crab. If conditions are right, local fishermen out of Bodega Bay, Point Arena and Fort Bragg put out hundreds of crab pots.

Dungeness Crab, *Metacarcinus magister*, looking awfully crabby.   Craig Tooley

Milkmaids, *Cardamine californica*.   Craig Tooley

Manzanitas continue to bloom, providing an early food source for our native Bees. A few Huckleberry bushes also begin to bloom, a promise of good things to come.

The lovely Milkmaids begin to flower later this month on the forest floor. They have two differently shaped leaves - a solitary rounded one at ground level, which appears first, and three-part leaves below the pink/white flowers.

Fun Fact: Milkmaids are also called Rain Bells and Spring Beauty.

This can be a great month for edible mushrooms. You might find Hedgehog mushrooms in Tanbark-oak and Bishop Pine forests, often under Huckleberry or Manzanita bushes. Black Trumpets begin pushing through the forest duff. Late Matsutakes along with Candy Caps and Chanterelles are still being found by lucky foragers.

Many non-edible mushrooms are also fruiting. It's fascinating to watch as they develop. Some Russulas actually form a chalice and hold rain water or a small, green Sierran Treefrog.

Hedgehogs, *Hydnum repandum*, Black Trumpets, *Craterellus cornucopioides*, Winter Chanterelles, *Cantharellus infundibuliformis*, and a Matsutake, *Armillaria ponderosa*.

Jeanne Jackson

A Wildlife Encounter with a Sierran Treefrog:

Have you ever heard of a frog making house calls? Al and Paula Kritz were hearing "ribbit, ribbit, ribbit" from every room in their Sea Ranch home. They finally spotted a Sierran Treefrog on top of the floor register close to their front door. His call was conveyed through the heating ducts.

They put him outside but he returned the next day, squeezing through the closed front door. Is it any wonder they named him 'Kermit'? They put him out three days in a row before bowing to the inevitable. He stayed several days, taking shelter under an umbrella stand and bringing much enjoyment to the Kritzs and their granddaughters, Suzanne and Rachel.

An early morning walk speaks to the simple joys of life. If you are lucky, you might spot River Otters climbing up a cliff or sliding down a riverbank. A River Otter has been seen sleeping on the south end of Schooner Beach, curled up against some driftwood.

River Otter, *Lontra canadensis*, asleep on the sand.   Nanette Brichetto

California's Coast Redwoods can live for more than two thousand years and grow over three hundred feet tall. Many of these trees were felled when much of the Mendonoma Coast was logged in the 1800's. Some were spared from the loggers because they were on private property and cherished more for their intrinsic value rather than their lumber. Others were spared because they didn't grow straight.

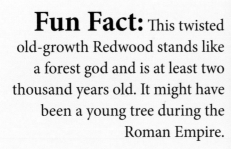

Fun Fact: This twisted old-growth Redwood stands like a forest god and is at least two thousand years old. It might have been a young tree during the Roman Empire.

Jeanne and Rick Jackson, along with their Golden Retriever, Huckleberry, are dwarfed by this Coast Redwood, *Sequoia sempervirens*.

Craig Tooley

The stars seem brighter this time of year. And as a storm passes by we are often left with showers interspersed with sunshine, blessing us with rainbows.

Double rainbow on the Pacific Ocean.

Craig Tooley

Cascades at Salal Creek.   Craig Tooley

February

Mendonoma Sightings Throughout The Year

Heavy rain followed by a day or two of sparkling sunshine is a frequent pattern in February. If you listen when you walk along a stream, you can hear many different water sounds. Yes, the stream could be singing just for you.

Sunsets through storm clouds give you a chance for a spectacular photograph or a lasting memory.

Sunset through storm clouds.   Craig Tooley

Between winter storms there is a space where warm weather can slide in. Daffodils will often bloom this month, only to see their hopes dashed and their sunny faces covered in mud from storms yet to come. Wildflowers begin blooming as if in defiance of winter. A few early yellow Redwood Violets tantalize us with thoughts of spring, as do Redwood Sorrel and Milkmaids. Yellow-blooming Acacias can be seen along Highway 1 and it feels as if you are entering an oasis of sunshine.

The ubiquitous Bracken Fern is beginning to send up fronds. This member of the Polypodiaceae family is edible but only when young and less than a foot high. Western Trilliums make their appearance in shady forests.

Western Trilliums, *Trillium ovatum*, in an old Redwood stump, along with Huckleberry, *Vaccinium ovatum*, Salal, *Gaultheria shallon*, and an emerging Clintonia, *Clintonia andrewsiana*.

Craig Tooley

Here's the Latin name of the Winter Chanterelle: *Cantharellus infundibuliformis*. It sounds like something Harry Potter would shout out as a magic spell. These edible, wild mushrooms will weave their magic around you this month, as they love the rain. Winter Chanterelles, or Yellow Foot, have a hollow stem, just like Black Trumpets. When dried they have the aroma of buttered popcorn.

Bellybutton Hedgehog mushrooms are often gleefully found, usually near Tanbark oaks. They are considered a beginner's mushroom as they are easily identified; there is no other mushroom like it. And, oh my, it is delicious.

Hedgehog mushroom, *Hydnum umbilicatum*, a delicious edible mushroom.   Craig Tooley

Turkey Tail Mushrooms, named for their resemblance to the male Turkey's mating display, can be found on downed tree limbs. Researchers are studying this fungus, as it may have significant medical qualities.

Fun Fact: Native peoples used this fungus as chewing gum.

Turkey Tail Mushrooms, *Trametes versicolor.*   Craig Tooley

This month can bring not only spectacular sunsets, but also beautiful sunrises. For a short time you may witness layers of pastel colors filling the sky and the Pacific Ocean appears to be liquid silver. Some days it pays to get up early.

The current off the Mendonoma Coast, the California Current, can deliver treasures onto our beaches. You might find a large glass Japanese fishing ball caught in the rocks at Bowling Ball Beach. These fishing floats have broken loose from fishing nets in Japan in years past. They go up around the Aleutian Islands and Alaska, and down the West Coast. If you are very lucky, one of these balls will wash up on a beach intact and you will have a treasure from the other side of the world.

A Mendonoma sunrise delights the senses.   Craig Tooley   Glass fishing ball.   Craig Tooley

Black Oystercatcher, *Haematopus bachmani*, standing on one leg.

Craig Tooley

Wildlife Sightings:

Sometimes a drive will bring you a plethora of sightings.

"*We saw large numbers of slow, southerly-moving Gray Whales who seemed to be dawdling and cavorting and spouting away or trying to tan their backs. Most sightings were in quite close to shore near the buoys, the farthest being midway to the horizon.*

"*At MacKerricher State Park we saw over 100 Harbor Seals hauled out on the shoals absorbing the sun, several Great Blue Herons eating fish in the low tide, huge flocks of local Gulls and Pelagic Cormorants, and a Black Oystercatcher in pink knee-socks in a mussel bed.*

"*We were fortunate to watch several Osprey diligently hunting in the Albion River channel and the biggest surprise of all were Cherry Trees and Daffodils in blossom!*"

—Grace O'Malley and Tim Winterer, Timber Cove

Fun Fact: Some birds, like the Black Oystercatchers, practice thermoregulation by tucking one leg into their breast feathers. This helps keep them warm.

Intrepid fishermen will be fishing when the weather allows. Thousands of pounds of Sea Urchin are harvested from our pristine waters. You may find Sea Urchin in a sushi restaurant under the name uni. Or better yet, you might see Purple Sea Urchins in a tide pool on the Coast.

Fun Fact: Sea Urchins have self-sharpening teeth and can chew through stone. They mostly eat algae. Sea Stars are in the same family as Sea Urchins. Both are sensitive to chemicals in the water so they thrive in the clean waters off the Mendonoma Coast.

Purple Sea Urchins, *Strongylocentrotus purpuratus*, and an Ochre Sea Star, *Pisaster ochraceus.*   Craig Tooley

And fishermen and women can be seen fishing for Steelhead on one of our local rivers if conditions allow. It's catch and release only.

Wildlife Encounter with a Steelhead:

Charlie Ivor is a fly fisherman and so he uses no bait, which makes the process of catching a Steelhead that much more difficult. But the reward when it finally happens is that much greater.

"*My fishing buddy, Tom Lane, and I set out to fish Alder Creek because we assumed that the rains would have blown out the Gualala and the Garcia. Upon seeing Alder, just slightly too muddy to try it, we drove back to the Garcia as the rains really started to come down.*

"*We fished and walked and fished and walked for several hours until I let out a holler that probably scared every animal in the area. This beautiful fish hit my fly like a freight train and battled me for enough time for both Tom and myself to scream and yell over and over.*

"*How lucky I am to have connected with this fish, to realize that because these fish are present we are in an aquatic habitat that is thriving and hopefully will remain so for eternity. After the picture, this approximately ten pound female was released and my day was made.*"

—Charlie Ivor, Gualala

Charlie Ivor with a ten pound Steelhead, *Oncorhynchus mykis*s, which he caught and then released.

Tom Lane

Spout of a California Gray Whale, *Eschrichtius robustus.*   Ron LeValley

Gray Whales continue to be spotted headed south.

Wildlife Encounter with Gray Whales, Sea Lions and Dolphins:

"*I had been watching Gray Whales and Sea Lions via binoculars from our house on Sea Ranch and decided to walk along the bluff to get a better view. The Sea Lions were very close and quite delightful. I was also intrigued by a pair of Gray Whales, because it looked like a mother and her calf – tall spout, small spout. So my dog, Jackie, and I walked along looking for spouts.*

"*I watched the Whales who were close to the horizon and the Sea Lions who were closer to shore. Cool. Then, as I'm looking through the binoculars, I realized that within the same frame of vision I can see both the Whales and Sea Lions. Very cool.*

"*Then suddenly I realize there is something in between the Whales and Sea Lions. I stare and stare, scarcely believing my eyes. Dolphins!!! I'm watching Whales at the top, Dolphins in the middle and Sea Lions at the bottom, all at the same time! Truly, truly amazing.*"

—Maureen Simons, The Sea Ranch

Fun Fact: Gray Whales rarely feed during the migration. They live off their fat reserves.

There's an unwritten Mendonoma Coast rule: always try and watch the sun set. There can be a possibility of a green flash. It's actually possible to see a green flash turn into a blue flash that then morphs into a violet flash, but that's exceptional. And if there is no green flash, you still have a lovely sunset to put in your memory bank.

There's another reason to watch the sunset. With the Coast's big-sky views and open spaces to the west, a Sun Pillar may appear. This happens when light from the sun is reflected off thin ice crystal clouds high in the atmosphere in a spot or band pattern vertically above the setting sun, an amazing phenomenon.

One of the rarest sightings can occur this month — a moonbow. Conditions have to be perfect. There needs to be a rain shower out over the water opposite the rising or setting full moon.

A Sun pillar is a rare sighting.   Jeanne Jackson

Moonbow Encounter:

"*I saw the most amazing thing last night! Jennifer Bundey and I decided to roast our dinner outside over the coals from a burn pile. It was about 7:30 p.m., the full moon was coming up and the stars were out, although there were some clouds and occasional sprinkles.*

"*We by chance turned away from the fire and faced the ocean and saw the most spectacular moonbow, a complete arch, spanning from Anchor Bay almost to Gualala, with each foot in the ocean. It was silvery, but very vibrant and clear, and we could even see some colors. I had never heard of such a thing before, but it surely was magical!*" —Emily Nelson, Gualala

Western Bluebirds are beginning to look for cavities to nest. Those who have put up Bluebird houses have been rewarded with an early sighting of these beautiful birds house hunting.

"Is it big enough?" Western Bluebirds, *Sialia Mexicana*, house hunting.

Craig Tooley

A Peregrine Falcon might be seen this month drinking water from the Gualala River or perched on top of a tree.

Fun Fact: Peregrine Falcons are the fastest birds on Earth. When swooping down on prey they have been clocked at over 250 miles an hour.

Peregrine Falcon, *Falco peregrinus*, resting on a branch.   Craig Tooley

A large antler was found on the ground at Salt Point State Park. Our Black-tailed Bucks lose their antlers every year and February is the time to look for them anywhere deer congregate. This shedding process takes two-to-three weeks and then the re-growth phase takes place over the summer. Bucks don't need their antlers now, but they will later on in mating season to impress females and fight off competition.

Antler present from a Columbian Black-tailed Buck, *Odocoileus hemionus columbianus*.   Craig Tooley

Once in a while the call of the wild will show us something that is not only uncommon, but surprising and fun, as in the following encounter.

A Mysterious Wildlife Encounter:

"*My wife, Sharon, and I started hearing an echo coming from the north side of the cove that sounded like someone pounding nails in a fence. Concurrent with that event I noticed a patch of beach with a trough of sand about six inches deep and about four feet wide scooped out with deep holes on either side. I deduced this to be a very large Sea Lion that came ashore and left.*

"*When the sound continued into the night I began to speculate, after a couple of glasses of wine, that it might be the ghost of a carpenter who constructed the lumber loading chutes 120 years ago at 'Bourne's Landing' on the adjacent bluff.*

"*Listening further on the next day I concluded that, due to the rhythmic pattern, it was some animal, perhaps the world's largest woodpecker? Finally the mystery was revealed – a huge bull Elephant Seal was in the cove emitting the sound as he stood up about six feet out of the water. This guy looks like a small whale with a trunk and I estimate he weighs up to three tons!*" —Allan Hemphill, overlooking Cook's Beach, Gualala

Male Northern Elephant Seal, *Mirounga angustirostris*.

Craig Tooley

Fun Fact: There is a web site where you can listen to different animal sounds, including an Elephant Seal. It's at partnersinrhyme.com. Use "ocean animals" in the site's search box to find the sounds you would like to hear.

Gophers, love 'em or not, are year round residents.

Wildlife Encounter with a Gopher:

"*Sitting on my garden bench gazing at the parade of Gopher mounds, I'm thinking, 'Climate change certainly hasn't affected the population of Gophers.' At that moment at my daughter Jenna's and my feet up pops the head of a Gopher. Is there Gopher telepathy?*

"*I tell Jenna that yesterday her dad fed the Gopher clumps of grass. She immediately started feeding it. The Gopher kept stuffing his cheeks and pulling clumps down his hole. Tiring of it, Jenna sat down and started talking.*

"*Suddenly alarmed, she jumped up and ran to get her year-old daughter, who was gently petting the Gopher on its head with her tiny, little finger. So much for Gopher traps! Guess I'll have to use planter pots.*"

—Gail Thompson, Gualala

A Pocket Gopher, *Geomyidae*, peeks up a hole.

Craig Tooley

Encounters with wildlife can bring joy in unexpected ways – even if it's a rascally Gopher.

Our most common Hawk is the beautiful Red-tailed Hawk.

Wildlife Encounter on a Drive to Point Arena:

"*We drove up to Point Arena between storms and it was quite an adventure. We saw Red-tailed Hawks and all kinds of birds in and out of the storm. While looking to see if any Tundra Swans were still around, we had hail and then wind and rain and sunshine. It was beauuuuuutiful.*

"*Going down into the Garcia River flats was like driving into a watercolor painting. The clouds, the fog and haze and then the clearness of the sky were such fun. We thought about going to the Point Arena Pier to look for Al and then the storm really came in. What an exciting day!*"

—Joann Harris, Anchor Bay

Red-tailed Hawks, *Buteo jamaicensis,* have distinctive screaming calls.

Craig Tooley

Later in February you may see the beginning of the northward Gray Whale migration as the first few Gray Whales with their calves glide by. And some of you might be fortunate enough to see a breach.

A Gray Whale, *Eschrichtius robustus,* breaches.   Kathy Bishop

Wildlife Encounter with a Breaching Whale:

Amanda Chase was driving on the Jenner Grade. She told her mom, Phyllis, "*I saw a whale! I saw the whole whale. I almost ran off the road!!*"

Yes, it's always a good idea to pull off to the side of the road to whale watch. And use those turn-outs to let faster vehicles go by. Watch for their friendly thank-you wave.

Birds begin migrating north too. Large flocks of Cackling Geese can be seen in the classic V just off the bluffs, making their distinctive high-pitched honking call. Low over the water in a rambling V you might see hundreds of Brant, a type of Goose, also heading north.

White-tailed Kites, a Hawk with a white head and breast, can be seen hunting in meadows. A trip to Brush Creek at Manchester State Park will give you the opportunity to see a Snowy Plover. Dogs are not allowed in this area of the park to protect these endangered birds.

Tiny Yellow-rumped Warblers overwinter on the Mendonoma Coast.

Fun Fact:

Yellow-rumped Warblers are affectionately nicknamed "Butter Butts." The "Myrtle" form of this Warbler is distinguished by its white throat. It is mostly found in the eastern part of the United States but has increased as a winter visitor to the Coast over the past decades.

Yellow-rumped Warbler, Myrtle form, *Dendroica coronata.*   Craig Tooley

Diminutive Calypso Orchids, *Calypso bulbosa,* can be hard to see.

Craig Tooley

If you take a walk in the rain you may see more early signs of spring. More Manzanita bushes are blooming, providing early nourishment for native Bees and Hummingbirds. Wild Strawberry, Douglas Iris, and Star Zigadene are beginning to bloom, along with the queen of them all, the Calypso Orchid.

Fun Fact: Calypso Orchids are also called Fairy Slippers.

Huge waves can batter the coast this month. The ocean might look like corduroy – no white caps, just big, steady swells stretched out to the horizon. The most experienced surfers are seeing if they are up to the challenge being laid down by the Pacific Ocean.

Seasonal creeks, full from the winter rains, create beautiful waterfalls as they tumble over cliffs.

Mist from the crashing waves drifts over Highway 1, giving it a dreamlike quality. Being on the Mendonoma Coast in February is a dream from which you won't want to wake.

The stormy Mendonoma Coast.   Craig Tooley

The grace of a forest.

Craig Tooley

Mendonoma Sightings Throughout The Year

As we contemplate the complexities and wonders of each month of the year, the unifying thread is the connectedness in Nature. We are part of that connectedness though it's easy to forget in the modern world. When we quiet the busyness, put aside the distractions, open our eyes – and, yes, pay attention – to the world of Nature that surrounds us, our lives are immensely enriched.

From the tiny Calypso Orchid that needs a fungus in the undisturbed forest to live, to the fascinating world of birds where the vast majority of them eat insects, to the Bobcats that hunt rodents, to the underappreciated Bishop Pine Trees that feed birds and other animals, to the majesty of the great Gray Whale migration, we humans need to be mindful of our impact.

Open your heart and mind to the intricate beauty that surrounds you. And in the quiet of a forest, Nature's cathedral, you can find peace and joy.

The iconic "bowling balls" seen at low tide at Bowling Ball Beach.

Allen Vinson

Cathleen Crosby – www.coastinghome.com

Chris Poehlmann – www.ChrisPoehlmannDesign.com

David Bergman-Hill

David McFarland

David "Sus" Susalla – Gualala Arts Center, www.GualalaArts.org

Deborah Heatherstone

Dennis Latona – www.pinenutz.com

Drew Fagan – www.drewfagan.com and www.dficreative.com

Eric Anderson – https://sites.google.com/site/abaloneten/

Jack Likins

Jacquelynn Baas

Kathy Bishop – http://kathleen-bishop.artistwebsites.com

Ken Bailey – www.seadreams.org

Lee Tate and Darrell Paige

Nanette Brichetto – www.nanbrichetto.com

Paul Brewer – www.capturingnatureswonder.com

Peggy Mee

Peter Baye – baye@earthlink.net

Rich Trissel

Richard Kuehn

Richard Lewis

Ron LeValley – www.levalleyphoto.com and
www.levalleyphotography.photoshelter.com

Rozann Grunig – www.Highway1Designs.com

Siegfried Matull

Tom Eckles – www.tomeckles.com

Tom Lane – flyguy@mcn.org

Featured photographer – **Craig Tooley. Email him at Ruffimage@gmail.com. Visit Craig's website at ruffimage.com.**

All photos within this book are by Craig Tooley unless otherwise noted.

NOTES